LIFE on the EDGE

For you, Martha,
Live well right
to the finish!

M. Steel

for you, Matthew
we will repay
to the amount
of $200

LIFE on the EDGE

Reflections on
Death, Loss, and Letting Go
from a Hospice Chaplain

SUZANNE BEA SLOVER LEAHY

Copyright © 2022 by Suzanne Bea Slover Leahy

All patient names have been changed to protect their privacy.

Cover Design by: Jen Casselberry
Editing and Formatting by: Casselberry Creative Design

Story Sanctum Publishing

ISBN: 9798848372274

In honor of Beatrice Mason Slover Krapf:
My aunt for whom I'm called, my dear friend and my inspiration.

ABOUT THE AUTHOR

To normalize and prepare for her own death, Suzanne has written her obituary and is including it here as a means for readers to get to know more about her life and background:

Suzanne Bea Slover Leahy was born three days before Christmas 1958 in Trenton, New Jersey. Her parents, Ray and Aggie Slover, along with her siblings, David and Nancy, had a very different holiday celebration that year! Suzanne grew up in Morrisville, Pennsylvania where she attended the Pennsbury Schools and Morrisville Presbyterian Church. She later graduated from York College of Pennsylvania with a degree in Psychology. Suzanne married and raised two sons, Jordan and Collin. While raising her children, Suzanne opened "Heartsong Breads and Spreads," baking yeast breads, fruit jams, fruit butters, the family's famous fudge and other homemade delights in her tiny farmhouse kitchen. One Christmas season saw Suzanne selling more than 120 pounds of fudge! Suzanne graduated from Westminster Theological Seminary in 2002 with a Master's degree in Counseling. In 2012 Suzanne earned a Master of Divinity from the same institution. While she loved being a homemaker and stay-at-home mom, her seminary credentials opened the door for her to begin a career outside of her home. Suzanne became passionate about hospice care when her dear Aunt Bea, for whom Suzanne was called, died of colon cancer in 1978. Auntie Bea's death guided Suzanne to a career as a hospice chaplain, where she met and cared for hundreds of wonderful people as they approached death. Suzanne's sons each found their perfect partner in their early twenties. Jordan married Lindsey and Collin married Hilary. Both daughters-in-law were a joy to Suzanne, not only as their sons' spouses, but as bright, creative, and loving women who contributed wonderfully to both their families and the world around them. In April of 2015 Jordan and Lindsey welcomed Ruby Day to the family, making Suzanne "Grammie." In November 2020 Ruby became a big sister when Hazel June was born. Both babies brought a new dimension of joy and delight to Suzanne. Suzanne continues to work as a hospice chaplain, where she feels most alive!

TABLE OF CONTENTS

Introduction: A Call to the Dying 11

PART ONE

Buddy and the False Teeth 17
Suzanne the Squeamish 23
Betty on the Stair Glide 31
Steven 35
Mr. Realtor 41
Hymns Around the Bed 45
Visit to the Crematorium 51
Kathy and the Baseball Bat 57
Brian 63

PART TWO

The Commonality of Cancer 73
Into the Operating Room 77
Angela 81
Hard Things 87
Sweet Anna 91
Death and Super Glue 95
A Sad Day for a Graveside Service 99
The Longest Funeral 103
In Their Own Sweet Time 107
I See Dead People 117

PART THREE

The Hollers 123
Death in the Trailer Park 127
Harold 131
The Paper Airplane Competition 137
James 141
Chaplaincy During COVID-19 147
Gretchen the Planner 151

Conclusion 159

INTRODUCTION: A CALL TO THE DYING

MY GRANDFATHER DIED rather suddenly when I was 9 years old. He was a fun grandfather who would do anything to make his grandchildren laugh. He used to come visit, most often as we had dinner, and tell us about his day. He would sit at the table with us and "twiddle" his thumbs, rolling one over the other continuously. He also warned my siblings and me to never eat peas saying, "They just roll off your stomach!" He and my grandmother took my siblings and me to the Carvel Ice Cream shop any time they had the chance, since they lived only about two miles from our house. There were lots of sleepovers, after which I would have to give Pop directions back to my house – I felt so important! He also let me and my sister play "Hairdresser" by putting pink foam rollers in the longer hair on top of his head, then using a floor lamp as a hairdryer. He was wonderful!

Then Pop had a nasty heart attack. My parents didn't give details and, while I knew it was a bad thing, it never entered my mind that he could die. But he did. I was mad. How could "they" let this happen? I wanted details, but none were given. A few days later, I and my siblings were given the chance to go see Pop before the funeral. This was my chance! I could find out exactly what was going on – where he was, what he looked like, if he had his red-rimmed glasses on, if he was comfortable. My siblings opted out, so it was my father and me.

We arrived at the "funeral parlor" as they used to be called, and I noticed three or four men busying themselves at a desk. They all looked old and pale, even gray, to me. No one smiled. I actually don't even remember them speaking, but rather just gesturing the way to the room where my grandfather was "laid out." I had no idea what to expect.

I followed my father into the room. At the far end was the casket. As we approached, I could see the profile of my grandfather and it was then that I realized he was really gone from us. I stood right next to the casket and checked his tie, his hands, his face, and wondered why he didn't have his glasses on. I had so many questions, but somehow knew questions were not allowed. I almost expected Pop to make the pre-tickle sound of rolling his tongue, but he did not.

After a time, we went home where more questions came to me over the next week or so. Questions about how Pop died, whether he could see us, why he was dressed in a suit and not pajamas if he was "resting," how he would be transported to heaven, why his wife (my Nana) could not get out of bed, and later, how people could go from being so sad at the church to eating and laughing at lunch afterward. So many questions for a nine-year-old, but somehow I knew I would have to find my own answers.

Just about ten years later, my dearest aunt was diagnosed with colon cancer. I was fortunate enough to be able to live with her until the point when treatments were not working. Hospice care was barely in existence where we lived and although we all did our best, the day came when Auntie Bea had to go to the hospital for care.

I watched her scan the house as she made her way to the door, and my heart broke. It was as if she was soaking it all in, memorizing every detail and knowing she would not return. Her son drove her to the hospital while her daughter made plans to leave her home in Tennessee to come be with her mother. It was a grueling time for me, but one that would inspire the rest of my days. I wanted to be sure no one had to leave their home to die if they didn't want to.

I visited Auntie Bea as much as I could, but back then hospitals had strict visiting hours. As the days went by, I also discovered the hospital had strict rules about pain medication. One day I asked a nurse for medication as my aunt was clearly in pain. She looked at her watch and responded, "Not yet." That's "just the way things were" and, as a 19-year-old, I had little power or credibility.

I struggled to find ways to encourage my aunt. Between her increasing sleep and the limited visiting hours, there were very few conversations. I wanted so much for her to know I loved her! Spring had come and I decided to dig up some crocuses from her yard. I put them in a pot and went to visit her. I put them right next to her bed so she could see them whenever she opened her eyes. Her daughter arrived from Tennessee and Auntie Bea was more alert than she had been for several days. This "rally" was short-lived, however, and a few days later she died – in the hospital, where visiting hours were strict, everything was on a tight schedule, and rules were rarely bent.

As I was headed to college in the fall to study psychology, I began searching out care models for people who were at the end of their lives. Without the internet my research was slow, but I was determined. In my junior year of college, I was able to do an internship at a newly opened hospice in my college town. I felt myself coming to life and knew this was where I wanted to be!

As any psychology student knows, graduate school is almost always in store if employment is expected! I knew I wanted to be a homemaker, spouse, and mother, so graduate school was in my fifteen year plan! I married and had two sons, all the while reading whatever I could find about the end-of-life experience and hospice in particular, talking with anyone from whom I could learn more and dreaming about working with dying people. When my sons were in their early teens, I returned to academia to earn a Master's degree in counseling and theology.

In the fall before my May graduation, a friend let me know of the opening of a chaplaincy position at a hospice in town. Although a full-time job and a full schedule at school would be difficult, I was determined. I interviewed for the position. After taking the phone call letting me know I had been hired, I sat in my car and cried. I had done what I could for my Auntie Bea, and now I could do so much more for other peoples' family members! This was the beginning!

PART ONE

1

BUDDY AND THE FALSE TEETH

AS I BEGAN MY CAREER IN HOSPICE fresh out of seminary, I thought I had to know all the intricate details of faith with which my patients did life. While there were some specifics which were, obviously, important for me to be aware of, I found that generally my patients longed for spiritual encouragement, prayer, and reassurance of God's love for them – denominations and philosophies became irrelevant. I met Mennonites, Native Americans, Muslims, Jews, Buddhists, and those from nearly every denomination of Christianity. Rarely did anyone ask me about my own faith. They seemed content to know I cared, that I was willing to listen to them, pray with them, and talk about their inner lives. Many times I read with patients, sang hymns with them, prayed with them. Sometimes we simply sat quietly. Sometimes we would laugh uncontrollably! The point was, I was there for whatever they needed and they began to trust me with their deepest thoughts and fears, the things they did not want to burden their loved ones with. It was during times of deep conversation, as questions were asked and answers discovered, that spiritual needs were being met. My own faith began to deepen and broaden as I saw others experiencing deep peace, hope, and even joy in the midst of the trials a life-limiting illness brings. I always felt my place was sacred, that of holy ground.

From the beginning of my work, one thing I found especially entertaining was the preconceived ideas of what a chaplain would be like and how the patient thought they should behave during our time together. These ideas often made me giggle, knowing myself as I do. For instance, most people thought they had to be very polite, not use "bad words" and certainly seem very interested in what I had to say. I loved to surprise patients by flashing one of the tattoos I have on my forearms! Their eyebrows would shoot up, jaws would drop and they would turn to the person accompanying them as if to find confirmation on what they were seeing! This antic seemed to be all the proof they needed that I was just a regular person; no halo, no secret cell phone connection to heaven, just someone who cared and wanted to be supportive. Often these first visits were the start of lasting connections, some of which I enjoy to this day.

Now and again, I would meet a patient who did not want to be cared for by a female chaplain. After attending a conservative seminary where women were not ordained to the preaching ministry, I was used to the perspective. With such people, I would ask them to meet with me

"...just to say hello and check in." Most often, that first meeting was followed by others, perhaps in the dining room or the comfortable lobby by the fireplace. Illness and disease have a way of clearing the fog of everyday life so we're able to see the most important things clearly. In time, patients would realize I was a safe person, one who could listen and give a genuine faith perspective. My only job was to ask good, honest, probing questions that would help that other person get closer to their own deeper feelings. Those were some of my favorite conversations!

Of course, there were patients and caregivers I met who had no faith background at all. It was never my job to persuade them one way or the other, only to love them and encourage them each time we met. During an initial visit with one patient, I asked if he had any particular spiritual background. He laughed and said, "I've never thought about God in my life. The way things look for me, maybe I'd better start now!" We went on to have many meaningful and positive conversations. Although he never specifically articulated a newfound faith, the peacefulness around him and the smiles and warm hugs spoke to a new understanding in his spirit.

I met another patient who had reportedly been very unpleasant with other staff members. I had been warned that he may not be receptive to "the chaplain" so I knocked on his door with some apprehension. As I knocked, I greeted him and told him my name – leaving out my job title! He barked, "What do you want?" I explained I was there to see how he was and if he needed anything. Just then he caught sight of my identification badge. "CHAPLAIN?! Oh no, you can leave right now! Go. GO!" I went! From then on, he kept his door closed and made it known that only nurses, doctors and housekeeping staff were allowed to enter. Anyone else could send information or messages through the select few allowed to talk with him.

My first post as a hospice chaplain was at a beautiful old Victorian house that had been renovated to accommodate about fifteen patients. Various businesses in the community had adopted a room and decorated it, so each room was different. A few rooms were more masculine, while others were more feminine. One room had a white picket fence along each wall with beautiful flowers of every color adding some cheer to the room. Hospice offices, the living room, dining room and kitchen were on the first floor. Patient rooms were on the second and third floors. The house was outfitted with a stair glide to transport patients from floor to floor. There was also a very large room on the second floor at the rear of the house specifically used for patients who were in those last hours before death. The room was large enough for many family members and friends to visit, as well as a sofa bed in case someone wanted to stay overnight.

In many ways this house was similar to being at home. Voices were heard, delicious smells of meals being prepared, music from the living room, birds outside the windows, and as much comfort as staff could provide. The house was a place of vitality, humor, peace, and joy, along with the intense work of dying. Many people wrongly assumed the house was a sad, tragic, dark place to be and I always loved sharing stories that made us laugh. Anyone who spent enough time there would learn and experience the balance of joy and sorrow, laughter and tears as we did life at its end together with our patients.

The director of the house brought her handsome golden

retriever, Buddy, to work every day. Buddy was still a puppy, but he was enormous! He would bound through the front door and up the beautiful winding staircase to wander and greet all those upstairs and, seemingly, announce the start of the day. Most people loved that dog, but a few did not. One dear woman, Amy, disliked dogs and would "shoo" Buddy whenever he came to her door. Still, he would tip-toe in, sniff a bit and gaze into her face before leaving and staying away the rest of the day. As Amy declined, Buddy would linger longer in her doorway. She would look at him and sigh, eventually not shooing him, but still delivering a glare which let him know he was not welcome.

Buddy had important work to do each day, encouraging, entertaining and just sitting with various people, including staff, so they could pet his soft fur and find themselves soothed. As Amy became unresponsive, Buddy seemed fully aware and attentive to her status. He made several stops by her room to check in, sit for a while, and then move on. One day one of the nurses watched as Buddy walked into Amy's room, circled the bed, then sat down beside it. He then nuzzled Amy's hand until it was over his snout! She would never have allowed this when she was alert, but there he was, keeping her company as she made her way from this earth.

Buddy always seemed to know when a patient was ready to die and he would station himself in or by their room. Amy's day was no different – he was right there for her and all of us as she left us. Buddy seemed to sense the shift, that she had died, and he stayed close. At one point, as I sat on a chair next to her bed waiting for the funeral home transportation crew, he came and leaned into my legs. That's when I began to cry. Buddy put his chin in my lap and let me hug his huge, furry body. I could hear Amy's voice in my head saying, "Get outta here, you devil!" to Buddy, but I think even Amy had come to appreciate the unique brand of love and comfort he brought.

One afternoon as I sat at my desk finishing paperwork, I noticed movement out of the corner of my eye. Staff "offices" were in the room once used as the family living room, complete with a fireplace. The room was enormous and allowed for several workspaces so each discipline could handle phone calls, charting, scheduling, or have an impromptu meeting together. A set of French doors divided the workspaces from the large entryway of the house. The movement wasn't unusual – people were coming and going all day – but something made me take a closer look. There was Buddy, jumping up, turning around, throwing his head back, running out of my sight and back again and generally having a dance party!

As I watched, I realized he had something he was tossing and chasing. Oh no, I thought. Apprehensively, I walked to the doors and opened one. Buddy froze. He knew he was in trouble. In his mouth he had someone's dentures!! He had gone upstairs, stolen the interesting item from a bedside table, and was having the time of his life playing with it! It was a situation where I wasn't sure whether to laugh or cry!

I snagged the dentures from him and went to find our director, his Mama. She was not happy. First we had to figure out whose they were, then face the moral dilemma of whether or not to replace the expensive teeth of a dying person who was no longer eating solid food. Needless to say, Buddy was banished behind closed doors for the rest of the day.

2
SUZANNE THE SQUEAMISH

AT ONE POINT IN MY EARLY LIFE I considered becoming a nurse. I loved science and the intricacy of the human body along with the idea of being able to give good care to people, so it seemed reasonable. It didn't take long before I realized nursing was a bad plan for me. First, there was a genetics class in high school where we opened fertilized chicken eggs at various intervals to observe their development. To this day I do not eat eggs! Then in college biology, we dissected rats – the white ones with little pink eyes. I have never been a fan of rats, but those little eyes haunted me! I took a nursing degree off the table.

Over the next several years I came to the solid conclusion that I was just too squeamish to become a nurse and settled on psychology.

Once out of college and raising my children, I had a terrible time caring for the various cuts and scrapes that inevitably came our way. My stomach would be in knots, then start to twist and turn. Next my head would start to spin, the sweat would bead on my forehead, and I would have to sit down before I fell down!

During a visit with my mother who had just come from the recovery room after a triple bypass surgery, I began to feel queasy. My sister looked at me knowingly. I tried to play it cool, while gripping the bed rail for fear of falling. The cardiologist happened to stop in to check in with us, took one look at me and said, "Oh, you need to come sit down here!" And to the nurse, "Will you please get this woman some water while I check her vitals?" How embarrassing! Along the way, I've learned to say, "If someone is sick don't call me! If they're dying, I'll be right there!"

Each week at the house we would have a staff meeting that included our medical director. The nurses would give a report on how their patients were generally doing, if they needed medication changes, and my favorite – wound reports. It didn't take long for my colleagues to notice my reaction to some discussions and then I was in real trouble. Every opportunity was taken to put me in a situation that involved blood, mucus, vomit, feces, skin tears, or anything they knew would make me squirm.

One day I was heading down the hall to see a patient when a nurse called from another patient's room. "Suzanne, can you give me a hand please?" The nurse was changing a dressing on a very large, very deep wound under the patient's arm. As soon as I stepped into the room, I smelled the terrible odor of infection and dying flesh. It was very strong and I really wanted to run, but of course I could not. I greeted the patient cheerfully and said to the nurse, "How can I help?" She winked at me and said, "You'll need gloves."

Wounds can happen quite quickly with a person who is dying because they are often bed-bound. The pressure of body weight on the mattress, poor circulation, incontinence, and fragile skin can all cause the skin to break down and open up into very painful wounds that can be difficult to heal. For this reason, a close eye is kept on skin integrity, with repositioning and dressing changes provided consistently to avoid such wounds. When all else fails, there is a handy little gizmo called a "Wound Vac" that does just what it sounds like it would. Tubing attaches to the pump which, when activated, uses pressure to remove exudate (fluids) from the wound. It was very effective. I just made sure I was never around when the time came to remove it and empty it!

That particular day, as I stood by this patient's bed and assisted the nurse, I learned a valuable lesson. I learned to focus on the patient's eyes and speak quietly, letting them know what was happening while at the same time making attempts to distract them with comments and questions about their room, their family, anything to take them away from the wound-dressing process. Most of the time, this plan of mine worked perfectly for both the patient and me! It was easy to look away from the wound site, but not so easy to avoid the odors of dressing changes, nor, for that matter, the odors accumulating during the dying process. After all, I had to breathe! Once a person has experienced those odors, I don't think it ever goes away. I always kept a container of a powder I liked in my desk and, when necessary, I would sit and sniff the powder to clear it away. It was a temporary fix.

Before I started working at the house, I had never followed the physical process of dying with anyone. Part of what I loved about being there was the ability to remain present for however much time a patient or family needed. The dying process, to me, is a matter of the body prioritizing what it needs to stay alive. Systems begin to slow down and fail. Hands and feet become cold, nail beds change to a blue/gray, dyschromia or mottling (skin discoloration) in the feet and legs begins as circulation slows, hunger and appetite are no more because the body requires so little fuel. Breathing slows, blood pressure goes down, heart rate increases and weakens.

Probably that most difficult thing to experience is what is often called the "death rattle," an accumulation of secretions that have built up in the back of the throat. As the patient breathes, a gurgling sound is produced. This combined with the slowing and inconsistency of breaths can be very stressful to witness. Of course there are medications that can ease these symptoms, and sometimes a patient will be suctioned for comfort. As death comes, breaths space out more and more until the next breath does not come. For me, there has always been a very real sense of peace after that final breath. I feel in my spirit the earthly struggle is over for that person and they can truly rest.

Families and friends, of course, respond in a million different ways and there is no way to anticipate what they will need at the time of death. No matter how much time there has been to prepare, death is an intruder. I have never met anyone who says, "Ah, ok. It's over. She's gone. I'm good." No one knows what it is like to live without a person they know and love, so when the reality of seeing that empty body comes, it is most often overwhelming.

Usually those present at the time of death will choose to stay with the body for a time. This is understandable and can be meaningful, but can also be problematic depending on the individuals! We had a spouse who completely fell apart upon seeing the lividity in her husband's body. Lividity naturally occurs after death. Because the heart is no longer pumping blood throughout the body, the blood pools and settles into the lowest part of the body. For this spouse, that lividity was more difficult for her than the absence of breath. She screamed at the top of her voice, "Make that stop!" As she tried to escape the finality of her husband's death, she would not allow us to call the funeral home to remove the body.

I had experienced this often, but never had anyone refuse for so long. Two hours. Three hours. We turned on the air conditioning. Four hours. By then it was very late and other patients were unable to sleep because of the sounds of crying and raised voices. Around the fifth hour, this wife agreed to the nurse making the call to the funeral home. We encouraged the wife by telling her she still had time, because it can take a while for the funeral home to arrive at the house. I suggested she wait downstairs while the funeral director and their assistant wrapped and moved the body onto the gurney.

Once they arrived, she slowly made her way to the living room. Surprising all of us present, the wife was calm and resolute. Someone made tea. We all waited together until her husband's body was brought downstairs. She accompanied him out to the funeral home van and waited as the gurney was loaded. Still emotional, she was crying quietly as she said one more goodbye to the man she'd married 27 years ago.

Back in the living room we finished our tea while she and the other family members shared memories and even a couple of moments of laughter. She seemed to have been able to calm herself. Memories of the previous years of illness and decline helped give her clarity and, as she left the house for the last time, she hugged me and said, "I'm glad his struggle is over." I knew then that, though it would take time, she would manage her grief and gain strength to keep moving forward.

Because of the age of the house, we often faced challenges when it came time for funeral directors to remove a body. This was a solemn time of saying a last goodbye, and the dignity of the patient and family were foremost in our minds. Sometimes a family would prefer not to come to say goodbye, and it was up to us to honor the patient. There is a fine line between honoring the patient and protecting other patients who are very aware their own death is ahead. Depending on the situation we might close the doors of other patients' rooms, but sometimes other patients would stop in the room to say goodbye. Sometimes our staff would gather in the front foyer as the funeral directors left. Now and then, someone would sing a verse of "Amazing Grace."

Many times, patients would die in the night and the funeral director would come and go with no one else but the nurse knowing someone had died. I was called in one such night and sat with the patient as he took his last breaths. We had loved this man because of his good humor, sharp intellect, and vast knowledge of movie trivia. He enthralled me often with details of movies I never would have noticed. As his body was removed, the funeral director and his assistant decided it would be best, given the location of his room, to go down the back winding staircase that led to the lower end of the parking lot. They had wrapped our friend in a sheet and then a soft blanket and used a canvas hammock-like carrier with handles on the edges to carry him out of the house.

As we made our way, the nurse and I began throwing out movie scenes he had explained to us. Before long, all four of us were laughing uncontrollably. At one point there was a misstep and the nurse cried, "Don't drop him!" The laughing stopped and we carefully continued our way down the rest of the stairs and out the back door.

On my drive home, I pondered the evening's details and realized a great truth. As our friend died and as we sent him off, we had honored him by enjoying what he had taught us. And as we laughed at nearly dropping him, I realized that even in death people must have their dignity protected and their lives honored. Surely, even if he had been dropped on that winding staircase, our friend would never have known. That wasn't the point, I realized. The point was to respectfully and lovingly see him on his way from us. I have carried that lesson with me until this day.

3

BETTY AND THE STAIR GLIDE

ONE OF THE MORE MEMORABLE PATIENTS at the house was a 76-year-old woman named Betty. She arrived in a blaze of glory, declaring herself the new "favorite resident." Some days it seemed impossible to believe that she had a life-limiting illness because of her energy, humor, sociability, and joy. On other days, the bad days, she would stay in her room quietly reading.

Some days Betty would plant herself in the beautifully appointed dining room and sip Constant Comment tea until the next meal, while she chatted with other residents until she wore them out and they returned to their rooms to rest. Betty had a way of making others feel they were the most interesting person she'd ever met. Her beyond-small-talk questions, her eye contact, even her body language communicated that she had somehow uncovered a treasure in the person she was visiting with. She only talked about herself when asked and would most often turn the conversation back to the other as soon as she could. This gave other residents the opportunity to share their lives and experiences at a time where most were engaged in "life review" in an effort to be sure the previous years had held meaning. Betty gave these dear ones the gift of her time and attention, which allowed them to uncover the gems of their lives and, usually, come to the conclusion that they had done well.

Betty always dressed in bright colors, wild patterns, dangly earrings and, often, mismatched pieces. She loved crazy socks and floppy hats. She had a zaniness that lit up her surroundings and encouraged the people around her. Betty was Catholic by faith as well as one of the more devout parishioners of her church. She had contacted her priest even before being admitted to the hospice to ask that he come visit and bring her the sacraments that would encourage her spirit and faith. Betty would invite other patients to join in these visits, which endeared her even more to all of us.

I often saw her kneeling by her bed, saying her prayers, as I walked past. We had many conversations about faith, from her Catholic perspective and my own Protestant perspective. She had an unshakeable trust in God's love and allowed herself room for unanswered theological questions. Betty just knew God's goodness, love, and care for her were real and it brought her deep peace. She often joked about how she must frustrate the Almighty with her general lack of decorum and the nearly irreverent familiarity with which she sometimes addressed God and various issues of faith. She always held rosary beads in her hands or had them tucked in her pocket.

Over the course of three or so months, Betty began to decline. She didn't come downstairs for meals or to socialize as often and she began using the Stair Glide instead of walking up the steps, but her spunk never left her. One day I was coming in the front door when I saw Betty on the Stair Glide, heading upstairs. I called hello and waved. She excitedly said, "Oh Suzanne, I'm so happy! Look what Father gave me!!"

As I approached her on the stairs, she held up a set of rosary beads that were unfamiliar to me. I smiled and said, "Oh, how nice!" She chuckled and told me, "They glow in the dark! This way if I die at night, God can't miss me!" Her words were a perfect statement of who Betty was – a woman of deep faith (God WAS coming for her!) and good humor. And, indeed, a couple of months later when Betty died, she had those very rosary beads pressed between her fingers!

Betty had made quite an impact on all of us and we missed her presence. As many as were able gathered one day to say goodbye. Her priest attended and we shared laughter and tears, but the resounding lesson we agreed on was that we had experienced a woman like no other. Her humor had lightened the atmosphere, and her deep faith taught, comforted, and inspired many. Her last months were as productive as any in her life and we had been blessed to spend them with her.

4
STEVEN

EVERY SO OFTEN, the hospice would admit a patient who had no insurance and no resources to cover the cost of care. Of course all such information was confidential, but once in a while things would go sideways and call for great creativity to provide what these patients needed and deserved without compromising their dignity. One such patient was a man called Steven who had AIDS. He came to us in a very weakened state after not being able to get out to buy groceries. He had been living on whatever his neighbors could drop off, which was minimally nutritious and inconsistent in arrival. There had been weeks where he would have only enough food for three or four days. The other days he would only have water and juices to drink.

Steven also arrived with the bare minimum of belongings – two pairs of threadbare pants and three shirts. No underwear, no pajamas. No toiletries. The hospice staff kicked into high gear and before long he had had a good, soapy bath, freshly brushed teeth, a clean hospital gown and a comfortable, cozy bed with clean sheets and warm blankets. Each time I stopped by to visit he was soundly sleeping.

As the staff got to know Steven, we discovered his favorite meals, snacks and desserts and made sure they were available as often as possible. At first he ate very little, but by his second week at the house he ate much more in quantity and variety. He even began requesting two scoops of ice cream as an evening treat! With the medical care, rest, nutritional support, and general tender loving care he received, Steven grew stronger and would venture down to the living room now and again. As I sat with him and we got to know each other, he trusted me enough to share his background.

Sometimes I could not hide my emotions and tears would slip down my cheeks. Steven had had a difficult childhood. He had received very little affirmation, encouragement, or direction. His family was quite wealthy. He had gone to college and graduate school, then worked at a high-paying job he loved. As an adult, life was good. Then he was introduced to heroin and everything changed.

Over the course of the following few years, Steven lost everything. Everything. Home, income, savings, dignity, family bonds, friends and, finally, his health. When he came to the house, he was truly broken. To make matters even worse, if possible, once he left the room he had been living in, some "associates" broke in and stole whatever they could find use for. When his landlord notified him of the theft, Steven had an interesting reaction. He sighed, shrugged his shoulders, and smiled. It was as if the very last aspect of his life had been taken from him. Now all he could do was simply focus on the day in front of him. He almost seemed relieved. He had absolutely nothing of his own, only things provided to him by our staff.

Steven had a few good months where he would spend time downstairs, either socializing in the living room, having meals in the dining room, or enjoying the beautiful wraparound porch as the weather warmed. I had spent a lot of time with him and had grown quite fond of his intellect, humor, and general perspective on life and death. He seldom mentioned spirituality or faith and I didn't push the subject. It seems that most humans just know when it has become important to consider (or reconsider) their thoughts on God and the hereafter. We had beautiful conversations and Steven asked deep questions as he probed his own heart and spirit, in search of hope and peace.

Soon our conversations turned to practical matters of "final arrangements," how Steven wanted his body handled after he died. He asked many questions and the staff found information and answers that satisfied him. He filled out a simple directive detailing how he wanted his last days to be handled and specifics of the cremation he preferred. Once those details were complete, Steven seemed to be lighter in his spirit, in the way he interacted with all of us. He laughed more and spent more time with others outside of his room.

All too soon for those of us who had come to love him, Steven suddenly declined. I would sit by his bed, read to him, pray with him, hold his hand, and sing to him. As he continued to fade away from us, the staff took turns being with him, making sure he was not alone. As it turned out, several of us were in the room when Steven died. We stayed with him for a time, hugged each other a lot, thanked God for our friend and, finally, the social worker went to call the funeral home for transport to their facility. She returned to the room with an odd look on her face. In reading Steven's chart she had found no funeral home listed to care for his body! This is an important part of any hospice admission and is rarely missed. But there we were.

Thankfully, this was during the day and the social worker was able to make a few phone calls to find a funeral home who was available to pick up Steven's body. About an hour later, after his body was bathed and dressed in a clean, soft robe, we said goodbye to our friend. The next day, the hospice director received a call from the funeral home's business office requesting payment for the cremation. This was not good! Steven had absolutely no resources from which to draw and the funeral director was not happy.

The hospice director called an emergency staff meeting to brainstorm ways of paying for the cremation. We talked about community organizations, civic organizations, churches, state funding specific to AIDS patients and anything else we could think of, no matter how remote the possibility of their assistance seemed. We divided the list and made calls for what seemed like hours. At the end, we had no funding.

Our director decided to give one more try to reasoning with the funeral home. It did not go well. The owner actually threatened to bring the body back to us! At that point, someone suggested we simply pool our money and pay for the cremation as a staff. In that moment it was as if the lights came back on after days without electricity – we had found one last thing we could do for Steven to preserve his dignity, even in death. The full amount was collected and delivered to the funeral home and everyone felt relieved.

A few days later, the funeral director came in the front door of the hospice with the familiar heavy black plastic rectangular box containing Steven's cremains. Not very sure what to do, we placed "Steven" on the mantle of the fireplace in the former living room that was now staff offices. At first, most of us would take a moment to stand next to the mantle, enjoying some silence and turning over private thoughts of the experience of knowing him.

As the days turned into weeks and then months and the pace of life caught up, we would stop by less and less. More than once the subject of Steven's cremains came up and we struggled with what to do. All these months later, I recalled a conversation during which he talked about the fact that he wanted his "ashes" sprinkled into the Atlantic Ocean, near Atlantic City if possible. What a dilemma! We knew we could probably never get everyone together who wanted to attend because of distance and schedules, and we knew the legalities of sprinkling human cremains into the ocean. It seemed impossible to fulfill Steven's final wishes.

In the end we decided to keep him close to us by sprinkling his cremains in one of the gardens at the house. We took some time one morning to share memories, thoughts, and lessons he had taught us. As we talked and laughed about our time with Steven, an old lesson dawned on me in a new way. The beauty and value he contributed to our lives, both staff and patients, had nothing to do with material goods. After all, he came to us with not even a toothbrush! But he had shared himself with all of us. He shared his experiences, his fond memories and current fears, his appreciation for things others overlooked, his own unique perspective. He left us all with a lot to think about and a lot to be thankful for. I still think of Steven now and again, when life seems to be an uphill climb. He still encourages me all these years later!

5

MR. REALTOR

THERE IS A COMMONALITY AMONG HUMANS. No matter where we live, who we are or how much we possess, the fact is we will all die. Most of us don't really believe or think about it until we're older, and sometimes people still try to figure out a way around death. We had one such patient arrive at the house as fall settled into the area.

Mr. Realtor was assigned a room that had been decorated with a man in mind with dark, earthy colors in the drapes and bed linens. He liked that his room was near the nurse's station. This man was very wealthy and well known in the community, having been in real estate for decades. By now his children were grown, grandchildren were in their teens, and the family numbered about 15. During his time with us, his wife visited three or four times a week, while the rest of the family came less frequently.

I stopped by on admission to introduce myself. Mr. Realtor stated he had no need of a chaplain, he was not a man of faith nor did he desire to become one! Of course, that was fine with me. I would stick my head in his door about once a week to say hello and he was cordial. One day several weeks after his admission, Mr. Realtor invited me into his room to sit in a rocker and chat. I was happy to do so and we had a long and interesting conversation about his life, his business, and his family.

After that day, I stopped by a bit more frequently to check in and let him know I was thinking of him. As he declined, he initiated a conversation about death and his own road to the end of his life. He laughed when he said, "Somehow I still can't believe I'm going to die!" He asked if I would stay with him nearer to the end, even if his family was there. I agreed. We talked about "final decisions" and he assured me there was nothing he needed to change. He was as prepared for death as anyone could be!

As it turned out, there was a significant snowfall the day Mr. Realtor died. I had arrived at the house in the morning and spent a lot of the day watching the snow come down from his window. It was a very peaceful setting. His family called, unable to get to the house because of the snow, and I held the phone to his ear so he could hear their voices. This would have to do.

Several hours later, Mr. Realtor stopped breathing. I waited. And waited. Finally certain there was no "next breath" coming, I went to tell the nurse. She came and assessed the situation, then listened to his chest to know if there was a heartbeat. There was not. I listened for myself. As I did so, I was overwhelmed with that same old feeling of being on holy ground. A life had ended.

I had spent so many years hugging people, hearing their heartbeats as I did so and being comforted by both. Now, in this moment, there was silence. It was an entirely new piece of evidence of death. The nurse called the family and his first son asked to speak to me. He thanked me for being with his father this evening and for the time I had spent leading up to it. I will never forget that night, that death, and that silent chest. It will happen to all of us. It will happen to me!

6

HYMNS AROUND THE BED

IT WAS A FAIRLY TYPICAL DAY in my life as a hospice chaplain. My patient had peacefully slipped out of this world leaving her husband of 46 years and their three children behind. They had lovingly cared for her for several years as cancer overtook her body, but now she was gone. It seemed the hard part was over. Or was it? As chaplain I explained that, when they were ready, I would call the funeral home and arrange to have them pick up their dearly loved wife and mother. Hesitantly, the daughter asked, "What will they do with her?" The conversation began to unfold and it was painfully obvious no one knew the "last wishes" of the patient. It was up to the family to piece together what they imagined she would want, and up to me to be sure everyone was heard and understood. It was going to be a long afternoon.

Sometimes families just don't agree on what is best for a loved one, especially if a patient has drawn up a Power of Attorney or Do Not Resuscitate order without their knowledge. As chaplain I was often called on to facilitate a family meeting to explore the wants, needs, and decisions of a patient. This was not a favorite aspect of my work! So, when Mrs. Green asked me to gather her children for a meeting, I was less than thrilled. But still, the family members who had come to visit Mrs. Green were pleasant, grateful, and very loving toward her.

The day of the meeting Mrs. Green appeared a bit nervous, so I asked how she was feeling. She said, "I just hope this goes ok. I just hope they all behave!" I felt a little twitch of apprehension in the back of my brain, but resolved that all would go well.

We chose a room at the back of the house for the meeting, both for its size and distance from others. We had bottled water and a plate of cookies set out. Everyone settled into the comfortable, overstuffed chairs, while I remained standing. I hoped this would give the signal that I was the facilitator and all conversation would be directed and civil. And it was. For about five minutes.

As requested, we began the meeting with a prayer during which I asked God for clear thinking, deep understanding, and love among the family members. Mrs. Green explained what she had done to prepare for her death and for the disposal of her body. There were raised eyebrows, crossed feet beginning to bounce, fingers tapping and a few sighs. I don't recall exactly what was said, but it was as if a bucking bronco burst through the gate! Everyone spoke at once, getting louder and louder with a lot of hands and arms flying for emphasis.

Mrs. Green stayed silent, so I took my cue from her. We waited. And waited. Finally, one of the daughters-in-law sat back down. That movement seemed to redirect the rest of the family. The volume began to settle and one by one, everyone sat down. What followed was a long but civilized conversation, a very emotional expression of grief at the coming death of their dear one and some very rational, helpful questions about what was ahead. In the end, Mrs. Green changed some details and her family had more peace about the weeks or months ahead.

About two months later, when Mrs. Green began actively dying, she was moved to the large room to accommodate visitors, of which she had many. Family scheduled visits so she was not alone and, as her time grew short, the entire family was with her. As I visited other patient rooms, I could hear the beautiful sound of voices singing some of the old hymns I had grown up with. I made my way to the end of the hall at the back of the house, knocked and entered the room. The room was full of people, some I had previously met and others I had not. Many were crowded around the bed where Mrs. Green appeared comfortable and peaceful. I can only imagine how it would be to hear those precious voices singing, comforting, reminding her of God's love and her hope of heaven. It was a beautiful experience for me. As I made my way into the room, greeting people, introducing myself to some, a few family members apologized for the behavior during the now infamous "family meeting." Of course, we agreed that the high emotions of that day were because of the deep love they had for Mrs. Green. I let them know that their family had taught me an important thing that I would be sharing with any and all future patients I would meet – the importance of having one's final wishes in writing.

Their singing continued and recurred over the next few days before Mrs. Green died. I imagined she was very happy and comforted not only by the singing and message of the hymns, but also by the fact they were all together and had not let differences drive a wedge in her family.

Most people do not want to think about their own death. I suppose that is understandable, but it is also a very important thing to work through and make known to people who will be caring for us in case of emergency. Certainly if we are diagnosed with a difficult disease, and as we age, it is very important to have these decisions made and recorded. This is not something to be put off until our later years, thinking it's unnecessary for young, healthy people. All of us face danger each day. I used to drive on a highway for work that was positively deadly! At least three times a week I thought I was going to be seriously injured or killed. That road was a main reason in my decision to take a different job and move! We can be as careful as possible, but we have no idea what anyone else will do that could end up changing our lives forever – or ending them.

It is important to have at least one person who is willing to be a Power of Attorney, so that if you are unable to make decisions and communicate, someone knows how you would want to be cared for. In many instances, this person is not a relative simply because the patient does not want the decisions to be clouded by a fear or dread of losing the patient. The person selected must be someone who loves the patient but is also able to exercise that love by carrying out the patient's wishes – even if it means death. Would you want to be placed on a ventilator? Would you want surgery? Would you want antibiotics? Pain relief medications? After death, would you want to be embalmed, dressed, made up and viewed by family and friends? Would you want to be buried? Where? Would you prefer cremation? What about the rising popularity of "green burial"?

While the topic brings up all sorts of emotions and feelings, it truly is a gift to your family to have these details settled. So often I have seen family members agonize over treatment decisions, removal of life support, funeral details and more. Many end up with a deep sense of guilt or, at best, uncertainty after they've made decisions. Dozens experienced regret over not having had a conversation to be aware of what their loved one wanted.

Hospitals and hospices have "Do Not Resuscitate" forms available at admission, funeral homes are happy to assist with pre-planning funeral details, and, of course, an attorney can be retained to draw up a Last Will and Testament, Power of Attorney, Medical Power of Attorney or whatever else is needed. Once that important information is recorded, a sense of relief comes and other more pleasant parts of life can have attention.

The Green family had a bumpy start to this process of death, but because of their love for their matriarch and each other, they came through without regrets or guilt. Certainly, we all want that for those left behind when we die.

Along that line, a few words about final decisions. I grew up in a little Pennsylvania town where everyone knew everyone. The funeral parlor was staffed by neighbors and people we knew from our daily lives. When funeral plans were being made, there was little question that the funeral director had the family's best interests in mind and finances were handled with gentleness, compassion, and the extension of credit! But times have changed. Many funeral homes are now owned by nationwide companies and their perspectives are different. Most often a family will be presented with options with a sales pitch about giving their loved one the best. The "best" is costly, of course.

As decisions are being considered and finalized, it is important to personally check the laws in your state for specifications on viewings, embalming, burial, "green burial," burial at sea and even home funerals as some aspects of body preparation are not required by law. These decisions are best made when the need is not immediate, but rather when there has been time to research and consider what is truly best and fitting for one's family. Although most people are reluctant to broach the subject of final arrangements, it is a gift to both family and other loved ones. There will be no guesswork, just the implementation of what was previously decided. I have heard more than one of my patients tell their family, "I made this plan to help you! If you don't follow it, I'll haunt you forever!"

7

VISIT TO THE CREMATORIUM

AS EXPECTED, family members have strong feelings about how a body will be handled after death, even when the patient has made plans for herself. They hesitate to talk about these "final decisions" for fear of upsetting either the patient or another family member. One afternoon, just such a family member came into the dining room as I sat at a table doing some paperwork. The room itself seemed to welcome conversation and offer warmth, with its pretty table linens, large fireplace, and walls the shade of butter.

Mike was definitely agitated and it concerned me. He had been through a lot in the previous 18 months. He had lost his job at which he'd worked for nearly 20 years, his wife filed for divorce, and his mother's cancer had returned with a vengeance. His face showed weariness and concern, so I invited him to sit with me. I asked what he was feeling and he went straight to the point.

While he was grateful his mother had made her wishes known, he was struggling with the fact that she wanted to be cremated and he did not know anything about the process. He was convinced "they stuff four or five people in there and we really don't know whose ashes we're getting back!" We talked about burial, which was his own preference, and the fact that he would have visible proof that his mother had been well cared for, since he would be able to see her body before burial. The unknowing was causing him great stress. Mike did not want to argue with his mother or upset her, but he was very conflicted. He asked me what I knew about the cremation process and I had very little to offer him. We talked a bit longer and I knew what I had to do. I had to contact the local crematorium and ask my questions.

The next day sitting at my desk, I felt a combination of curiosity, excitement at learning something new and practical, along with a sort of heaviness to be confronting something so real, so intense. I prayed for courage, took a breath, and dialed the phone. The man who answered was very personable, introducing himself as Bob, and eager to be helpful. I introduced myself and he quickly responded with, "Oh yes, we've taken care of a lot of your patients!" Somehow this was reassuring to me. I went on to confess my lack of knowledge and understanding of the cremation process and he eagerly invited me for a tour of the facility. I accepted, set a time for the following day, and thanked him.

When I arrived at the crematorium I rang the doorbell and waited, secretly thankful it wasn't a "walk-in" situation. I was apprehensive about what awaited me on the other side of the door. I recognized the man's voice as the one I had heard on the phone the previous day. Bob was pleasant and conversational and I couldn't help thinking he was just happy to spend some time with a living person who would respond to his comments! He jumped right into the tour showing me his office, the entry, the huge refrigerator with shelves down either side, and stacks of flattened cardboard boxes that opened into the required "container" to hold a body as it goes into the retort, or cremation chamber.

From there we went into another smaller room and I had the feeling things were about to get more specific. Along one wall were two very large metal doors each with a heavy handle and various knobs and gauges running down a panel on the side. While the first room had been very quiet, this room held a loud and constant, "Hhhuuummmmm."

Bob told me that the two doors were those of the retorts. My mind filled with questions! How did the casket, either wood or cardboard, move into the retort? Was the family allowed into this room? What was the temperature of the retort? How long did it take to cremate a body? What happened when the process was finished? Were there ever times when ashes were not claimed and what happened then? And, of course, the question that started it all, how many bodies are in a retort at once? As my questions swirled, I noticed that Bob was reaching out toward the wall, then I realized he had pushed a button on the retort. Just then the heavy metal door began to rise and I took a sudden gasp of air – I had no idea this would be part of my tour! As the door rose, curiosity took over logic and I bent to look into the retort. One question was immediately answered: only one body fits into a retort at a time.

I stood for a few seconds taking it all in, then stepped back. I had seen the conveyor-like track that moved the casket into the retort and had seen the space inside. I took another look around this room, then followed Bob out of this room to our starting point. I asked Bob more questions: Was a family allowed to be present for the cremation? Bob told me that they were, indeed, allowed inside and often pushed the necessary buttons themselves. He continued on, knowing I probably had the same questions as many others had had for him.

The retort can reach a temperature of 2,000 degrees and the process can take two to three hours to complete. What is left are actually bone fragments, which are then pulverized into what most people call "ashes." As we stood next to the exit end of the retort, there was a large metal garbage can next to the pulverizer. I looked in to see an odd, tangled mess of metal joints, steel rods and other metals. These had to be removed in order to process the bone fragments. Once complete, the remains (often called cremains) can weigh between three and nine pounds, depending on the size of the individual.

On a nearby shelf, Bob pointed out the plain, black plastic box into which the cremains were put. The box was lined with a heavy plastic bag, just to be sure to keep the cremains contained. The box was then sealed and labeled with the decedent's name and date of death. Bob would then call the family and someone would pick up the cremains.

Occasionally, the cremains were abandoned, not picked up by anyone. In this case most funeral homes and crematoriums will store the cremains, along with careful records, in hopes that someone will call for them. In extreme cases, cremains may be buried in a common grave. Some states in the US allow for the scattering of ashes after not being claimed for 12 months. Wow. I had learned so much and was glad I could now say with authority that I knew how cremations were handled.

A couple of days later the patient's son, Mike, came to visit. I was able to flag him down before he made his way upstairs to see his mother. I told him about my visit to the crematorium and all I had learned. He laughed, not realizing I would actually go to the crematorium for answers! I confessed I had gotten more than I bargained for, but what I learned would help many other people down the road. Thankfully, Mike was able to work through his apprehensions and agree to abide by his mother's choice. When the time came, Mike chose to say goodbye to his mother at the house and have another family member pick up the cremains when they were ready. Mike had peace and his mother was given what she wanted.

8
KATHY AND THE BASEBALL BAT

MOST EVERYONE HAS HEARD or read about the stages of dying and grief. Our emotions are what make us unique, make us human. Our emotions help us express ourselves, help us cope with things, and generally make sense of the world. Some people are very "in tune" with their emotions while others try to ignore unpleasant emotions by stuffing them inside with drugs, alcohol, shopping, excessive exercise, food, knowledge, and many other things. The trouble with this "stuffing" is, things can only stay down so long before something cracks open and everything pours out. This can be very destructive, even fatal. It can be very difficult to explore our emotions with someone else. We make ourselves vulnerable to that person's response and if that response is not positive or helpful, it can be devastating.

When Kathy came to the house, she appeared confident, bright, positive, and cheerful. She settled into her room and made it her own with pictures of family and friends close by the bed. She had the bed moved so she had a better view of the door. And then she settled into the rhythm of the house: the timing of meals, visitors, activities. I enjoyed getting to know Kathy. She, like I, had been a stay-at-home mom for many years. She loved cooking, baking, gardening, and even ironing (it's hard to find another who enjoys ironing the way I do!). She loved the feeling of sweat running down her back after a good workout and was a self-described bibliophile! I liked her so much.

At first our conversations were typical getting-to-know-you talks. She was easy to be with and seemed to have a good handle on her situation. One day, though, something was different and I couldn't put my finger on it. Kathy seemed agitated, antsy, words coming a mile a minute — so fast I couldn't grasp what was happening with her. She finally took a breath. The room was still. I waited. After what seemed like an hour, Kathy looked at me and said, "I'm just SO angry! I'm not an angry person, I don't know what to do with this!" It made sense to me. Kathy was a bright woman who had had a very organized life until her diagnosis. At that point, most everything she had in place was tossed aside to accommodate treatment, then the realization that she would not survive.

The entire situation was unacceptable to her and she just didn't know how to cope. She had always been able to manage difficult situations, but this was beyond human control. All that could be done had been done and the result was the same. And she was angry! The rest of that day and the next, Kathy preferred to stay in her room and I poked in to check on her several times. She seemed to be working things out with her journal close at hand and her favorite hot cocoa on the bedside table.

The third day, she seemed more interested in conversation. We talked for a while about where she had been in her life, how she had spent her days, what "counted" and what didn't. Of course, I had no answers for her – it was my job only to listen and ask thoughtful questions to help her continue to explore her feelings. I must say at this point, it can be very tiring to have these conversations. They take great energy, thought, and focus to stay with the other person while also knowing when to take a break. Often people are confronting issues from their past or things they've long buried. Looking at these things while also being physically weak is difficult at best.

A few days later I poked my head in and said good morning to Kathy. She responded, "Oh! I'm glad to see you! I know what I need to do!" This was music to my ears as I made my way in and sat on the edge of her bed. Kathy excitedly told me she had been thinking, journaling and arguing with God about her prognosis. All to no satisfactory resolution. Nothing she could do would change things for her. She was just down-in-her-gut ANGRY. I was a bit perplexed because she seemed to be ok with her conclusion, so I asked, "So, how can you keep moving forward emotionally?" She smiled the widest smile I had seen on her face and explained what she wanted to do. She wanted to find a plastic baseball bat and "beat out the anger!" I laughed with delight! The idea of seeing kind, petite, proper Kathy swinging a bat in anger was something I didn't want to miss!

Unknown to me, there was such a baseball bat kept in the downstairs office for just such a purpose! It had not been put to use since I arrived at the house, so it had never come to mind as a solution for Kathy. I told her about the bat and we began planning. She wanted me to be there and she wanted to use the room toward the back of the house, the one with the comfy chairs and the large, pillow-lined sofa. She asked me to gather more pillows "just in case!" We planned the session for the next afternoon and I let the staff know what was happening, in case of loudness.

The next afternoon I went to Kathy's room and found her dressed in stretchy pants and a loose t-shirt. She smiled broadly and said, "I'm ready!" Once in the room she asked me to pray for her, which I did. I asked God for clarity, courage, and a bit of resolution. Kathy held the bat for a time and then slowly raised it. The first few whacks were unimpressive, as if she was waiting to see what might happen to her if she expressed herself. I quietly asked, "How old are you, Kathy?"

The simplicity of the question apparently had a significant effect on her, because she began hitting the sofa with more force, then faster and faster. She called out by name things she would miss because she would die at this age, called out the unfairness of having done things "right" only to be slapped with disease, then the fear of facing something no one could share with her. As she slammed away at the sofa and pillows, I could see her strength dwindling but she continued. So much anger, so many unnamed emotions came out, but she seemed determined.

After what seemed like hours (but was really only about 25 minutes!), Kathy placed the bat on the floor and slumped onto the sofa.

We were quiet. She drank some water. It didn't seem like the time to ask her how she felt, so I didn't. After a time, she took the Stair Glide and I walked with her to her room. She badly needed a nap!

The next day when I checked in with Kathy, she thanked me for being with her the day before and I thanked her for allowing me to share that sacred time with her. I asked how she was feeling since then. Her response was really very wonderful. Kathy said that she felt relieved to have a lot of negative feelings "outside" of her, but she had come away from the experience with the same reality – she was going to die and she was still angry about that. She talked about how she had lived her life, year after year, choice after choice, doing what she thought was best for her and her family. She wouldn't change anything.

Somehow this diagnosis was as much a part of her life as anything else had been – where she went to college, who she married, the seemingly mundane issues of every day. This was her life. This was how her life would end. This was the time to decide how to spend the day in front of her because she might not feel as well tomorrow. I don't think I could have wished a better realization for Kathy, and it was certainly a lesson for me, too.

As both of us moved from day to day, I found myself more deliberate in the way I spent my time, the things into which I invested my time. And Kathy did the same. She spent time with the other residents, lingering after meals to chat. She spent time on the beautiful wraparound porch and she spent time making phone calls to people she needed to speak to. Her family came often and she proudly introduced them to anyone they hadn't met. She spent her days giving to others while, at the same time, asking for what she needed, too. She often asked me to pray for her, often asked someone to just sit with her until she drifted off to sleep, asking for certain music in her room.

And one evening, she died peacefully with her husband and children beside her. I think of Kathy often. She taught me that it's ok to express those feelings others define as "bad" and it's ok to ask for help when we need it. She showed me in a new way that it's ok to acknowledge our feelings and face them. It can be liberating. It can be life-changing. And most importantly, we need not wait until we have a life-limiting diagnosis to deal with our feelings.

9

BRIAN

FROM THE BEGINNING of my interest in hospice care I had avoided the reality of children who might need it. Although I read a bit on the subject, I always hoped and prayed I would not be needed in a family where a child was dying. Then one day, my director came and sat next to my desk. She had never done that before, so I knew I was either in deep trouble or about to be asked to do a difficult thing. I wasn't excited about either option. When I looked over at her face, I knew I wasn't in trouble – it was worse. As she explained it, a seven-year-old child, Brian, had been struggling with a rare cancer. His parents also had a younger son and their mom was expecting a new baby in five months.

The last round of treatments had left him very weak and had had no impact on the raging cancer in his little body. They were a family of strong Catholic faith and prayer had been a part of Brian's life for as long as he could remember. He knew many, many people around the country were praying for him to get well. So when Brian heard the treatment was not doing much more than making him miserable, he told his parents he didn't want to do any more treatments.

He was tired of being in the hospital, tired of needles, tired of feeling so terrible and tired of not being able to see his dog, Scamp. He just wanted to go home. And so, his parents honored his request and began planning his discharge from the hospital. The hospital social worker called several hospices to see if they would take on Brian's care. The answer was always "no." And then she called my tender-hearted director and told their story.

Pediatric hospice care is, of course, very different than that of adult care, but we happened to have a nurse with pediatric hospice care experience. A staff meeting was called to discuss Brian's case and even though no one was very eager, it was decided we would take him on. About two weeks after Brian's admission, my director came to my desk. She asked me to do a morning shift with Brian so his mom could take his little brother to nursery school, grocery shop, and then pick his brother up from school and come home.

My first morning with Brian was a whirlwind of emotions. I chose to focus on the tasks at hand and deal with my emotions later. By now Brian was in a hospital bed in the family living room, a room flooded with light, green leafy plants and two comfy sofas. Also there were three bean bag chairs for young visitors and big floor pillows to flop on. The wall by Brian's bed displayed artwork done by his brother, friends, and cousins. He especially liked the drawings of his favorite cartoon character from "Blue's Clues."

Little brother, John, was quick to warm up to me and eager to introduce me to his brother. Brian was very weak, but he smiled and said, "Hi." I told him I was happy to meet him and I would keep him company for a while. Again, a weak smile. I couldn't help but love this guy!

Mom gave me detailed instructions about what to do if…, then shrugged and smiled saying, "You'll be fine." As she went out the door, she hugged me and said, "Thank you." It was one of the most heartfelt thank you's I ever received. I was amazed by this mother's strength. Strength that allowed her to have her dying son at home, strength that allowed her to keep life as normal as possible for her younger son and strength to leave her beloved, fragile child with a woman she had only just met. I knew my time with this family would be profound and have a lasting impact on my heart.

Once Mom and brother left, I went back to sit with Brian. He looked so comfortable in his bed with cartoon sheets and soft, fuzzy blankets. I asked if he would like to read a book and showed him my personal favorite book I had brought along, *Robert the Rose Horse*. His eyebrows shot up and he said, "I've never heard of that book!" So it was decided. For those unfamiliar, Robert is a horse who becomes allergic to roses. The doctor tells his parents he must go live in the city to avoid the roses that grow everywhere in the country. Each time Robert comes upon a rose, there is a giant sneeze. I am very good at overemphasizing that sneeze over and over through the story. Brian would giggle with every sneeze, so it was well worth the silliness of emphasis! Brian soon began to drift off to sleep and I promised we'd read again later. I sat next to him and watched him as he slept, hoping his dreams would take him somewhere wondrously carefree and beautiful.

Before long, Mom and John returned. John ran straight to the living room to show Brian his schoolwork. I loved the way Mom allowed John to interact with his brother, even when it meant waking him from a nap. As she explained to me, she did not want John to ever feel he could not talk to his brother, because there would be the rest of his life for that once Brian died. We chatted about "normal" things for a bit and then I went on to work. I had securely stuffed my feelings and thoughts deep into the recesses of my heart, which was the only way I could still give care to the other patients I was scheduled to see.

By the end of my day, I had decided to take the long route home to allow myself some debriefing before I arrived home to my family. As I drove through the countryside lined with horse farms and hay fields, I decided I had better begin by praying. I asked God to be my peace, my courage, my strength, and my wisdom as I walked toward death with this dear family. God's answer was almost immediate as I began to realize what a beautiful opportunity I had been given! I had been tasked with offering real life responses to what has to be one of life's most horrible situations. The quick and ultimately meaningless answers would not do at all. I had to be paying attention to both the family and their faith. I had the beautiful challenge of directing to God those who would struggle with both seeing and trusting him in the weeks ahead.

My visits with Brian became less interactive as he began to sleep more and more. When he slept, I would read from the book of Psalms, sing songs and pray for him. I loved those times while, at the same time, knowing they would soon end. Soon Brian was unresponsive and his parents decided it was time John stayed home from school. I wondered how they knew, but rather than ask, I chalked it up to loving parents knowing their children and each other well enough to know they wanted to be together every moment possible. They asked me to keep coming to the house to be with them, which felt like such an honor, a gift to me. It seemed like each time I arrived there were more people there – grandparents, cousins, aunts, uncles, neighbors, friends from church and on and on. Somehow the house always held the wonderful fragrance of coffee and something baking! I know it was purposefully engineered for Brian, but the rest of us certainly enjoyed the coziness.

Then one morning I arrived a bit early to find very few cars parked near their house. This might have meant two things: either Brian was better today and others didn't feel the need to be there, or he was much worse and others were giving the family their privacy. Somehow I knew it was the latter. I said good morning to little John in the kitchen then moved into the living room. All four grandparents were there, along with Brian's parents. They all looked weary, but smiled just the same.

I went over and said good morning to Brian, snuggled him and kissed his very warm cheek. His breathing had changed and slowed and experience told me there wasn't much time left. I turned and asked one of the grandmothers what her favorite memory of Brian was. I honestly wasn't sure if that was a good thing to do or not! I didn't want to stir up more emotion than necessary, but I also wanted them to remember more than cancer and what was happening this day. It turned out to be a very good thing and the other grandparents joined in with, "Remember when…" for the next 90 minutes.

At one point John came in and said, "What's all the laughing about?!" As the day wore on, the grandmothers made lunch and they asked me not to leave just yet. The truth is, I never wanted to leave. This was a place of deep faith, of love, of peace, of understanding that God can still be good when terrible things happen. I stayed. As the afternoon wore on, Brian's respirations became fewer with more time between each.

His mom laid in the bed next to him and his dad sat next to the bed. John understood that Brian would soon be gone and he buzzed in and out as any four-year-old would. Late in the day, but with the sun still shining, Brian died. The stillness of the room was somehow comforting as we stood around his bed. The peace was precious, a kind of peace I had not felt in a very long time, if ever.

Brian's dad asked if I would pray, so we all joined hands as I prayed a prayer of thanks for the dear little boy he had given and now taken back to heaven. I asked God to be everything this family would need in the next few days, and well beyond. Suddenly we all heard a little voice saying, "I NEED TO GO POTTY!!" We broke into laughter as a grandmother ran off to help John. It was a bit of seriously necessary comic relief!

Before long, Brian's dad called the funeral home and asked them to come for Brian. Everyone had been dreading this time and all too soon the funeral director himself arrived. When they decided to bring Brian home, Mom and Dad had gone to the funeral home to make plans and discuss this very moment. The funeral director was very kind and compassionate and, when the time came, Dad was the one to wrap Brian in his favorite blanket, carry him to the hearse and tuck him in on the stretcher. There was no holding back tears for the rest of us. Such a tender, heartbreaking scene. Once again I had the feeling of being on holy ground.

Brian's funeral mass was held a week later and the church was full of people who loved him and his family. Several dear friends spoke of the family's faith, their strength, and their love for each other. One man asked everyone present not to forget "a few months from now" but to stay close and check in on the family, especially as the new baby arrives and brings a whole new level of emotion. The last person to speak thanked Brian's mom and dad for their transparency over the course of Brian's cancer. He talked about the way they never presented a false positivity, but outwardly and openly shared their feelings of fear, anger, dread, resignation, futility, and helplessness. They had been faithful teachers to many, he said.

As I listened to all the voices, I felt such gratitude at having been involved with Brian's death. While it certainly wasn't anything I would have volunteered for, by the day of the funeral I was very grateful for having been there. So much beauty amidst what is surely a nightmare every parent hopes to avoid. Having been given no choice, Brian and his family spent the last months of his life teaching others how to genuinely care for people who are suffering. People had been changed for the better by their choice to live honestly in front of them. Such a gift.

PART TWO

10

THE COMMONALITY OF CANCER

A FEW YEARS WENT BY and I found myself faced with an offer to work in a treatment facility for cancer patients. It was an interesting offer. Higher salary, no community visits, new things to learn, new skills to sharpen. I took the chance and accepted the offer. From day one I was glad I had made the move. Of course I missed my colleagues and the atmosphere of the house, but this facility offered all sorts of challenges and opportunities that I found very exciting.

When a new patient was admitted, they were scheduled to meet with each discipline offered in the center. This allowed an opportunity to learn about the support available and meet various staff members. I, as Chaplain, was scheduled to meet with them and talk about the spiritual support available. I often came across the same responses as during my years at the house: very polite, no "bad words," surprise that I wasn't a man, pleasant expressions, and lots of nodding!

I always began these meetings by saying, "I'm not here to beat you over the head with any one version of spirituality!" Eight times out of ten, that created a lighter atmosphere in the room. My role, once again, was to determine how the patient was coping with their diagnosis, what role faith had in their lives and let them tell me how to best support them and their caregiver(s). This required a lot of probing questions, balanced with general conversation about their lives and experience with cancer so far. I learned so much from these meetings and I honestly approached each appointment as a 30-minute treasure hunt! I met people from every faith group I could think of, and some I had not.

Over the course of their treatment, my patients were gracious enough to share their lives with me and teach me things I didn't know about their own faith practices. I was once visiting a Muslim patient when her son arrived home from work. He greeted me but did not make eye contact. I thought perhaps he was simply tired and emotional over his mother's condition. As we chatted, the young man continued to look at the floor. Once I was back at the office I began reading and discovered that, because of the tenets of his faith, it was improper for him to make eye contact with me. Among those of the Catholic faith, for many years cremation was not "allowed" by the Church. More recently, things have eased and cremation is no longer forbidden.

As in my previous experience, denominations disappeared and the one-on-one connection with God was priority. We had a lovely chapel in the facility and it became a haven for many. We had morning prayer to start the day, classes on various topics and always an available ear for those wanting support. In that chapel we baptized, celebrated marriages and anniversaries, celebrated Hanukkah, decorated a Christmas tree, had a Catholic priest apply ashes on Ash Wednesday, we cried, we laughed, we said goodbye and we said hello. So many lasting friendships were born, friendships based on the commonality of cancer. One woman told me she hated cancer, but she was glad for all the good things that came into her life because of it!

11

INTO THE OPERATING ROOM

A YOUNG WOMAN CAME TO THE FACILITY to be treated and I could see from the start we would be friends. Although she was younger, we had many similar interests. Barb was a woman of strong faith, and praying together was a part of our everyday routine. She was very brave, but when it came time for her to have a port surgically implanted in her chest, she became anxious. A port is used to draw blood and give treatments. It can also be used for blood transfusions and medications. It is placed in the operating room just under the skin on the chest and basically allows a patient to avoid being continually stuck with a needle. It also allows for treatments that last longer than a day and a double port allows more than one medication to be administered at the same time.

Once treatment is no longer needed, the port is removed.

Barb was terrified of the surgery ahead of her. The procedure had been explained by the surgeon, a couple of nurses and other patients who already had had it, but she was still fearful. Then she asked if I would go with her. I was confused– go with her where? INTO THE OPERATING ROOM!! Remember, I'm the squeamish one! I was in trouble. Then I thought, there was no way the surgeon would allow me into the operating room, so I felt some relief. Then the surgeon AGREED to have me in the operating room for the quick procedure. I was in BIG trouble!

He met with me, giving instructions and describing the procedure. Most important, he said, was that if I felt "woozy," I should immediately sit down. The day of surgery, I stopped in to visit with Barb and pray. She was unusually serene, for which I was thankful. She thanked me for being with her during the procedure, having no idea I dreaded it more than she did! I took instruction on "gowning up," which involved much more than just a gown, before entering the operating room. I had thought it all through and decided to simply focus on Barb's face and ignore all else. It worked perfectly and the only problem I had was when I reached out to touch Barb's arm to soothe her with my blue-gloved hand. "Sterile field, Suzanne! Sterile field!!' I could see the surgeon's eyes crinkle in a concealed smile as I snapped my hand back. Much sooner than I expected, it was finished. The procedure went perfectly, Barb was resting and I went back to the chapel to breathe.

I had a lot to think through. I was thoroughly amazed and impressed by the surgeon's abilities along with his fun and compassionate "bedside manner." His support team was equally impressive, communicating succinctly and speaking kindly to the patient when she arrived in the operating room and once she was in recovery. But the one thing that kept buzzing in the back of my mind was, why did Barb want me IN the operating room when she would be under anesthesia? I could walk her to the door, then be beside her in recovery when she awoke, so why was she insistent I be next to her during the procedure?

As I came to understand, Barb lived a rather isolated life. She interacted with a small handful of people at her church, but even those friendships didn't go beyond surface issues; they were not "doing life together." Barb was fearful of being on her own at such a critical point in her life, but she was facing her cancer diagnosis with very little support outside of the hospital.

As I thought through her situation, it became very clear that she had become a casualty of this modern day – busy, busy, busy all week, catching up on the weekend with a quick stop at church on Sunday. A schedule like that does not allow much room for friendships or building a support system. I was thankful for this lesson which was a reminder to me not to get stuck on the treadmill of life, but to make time and space for other people who can encourage, strengthen, challenge, and support me as I move through my life. I was, and continue to be, grateful for the lesson, although I could've done without the operating room!

12

ANGELA

IT IS ALWAYS DIFFICULT to see any person deal with cancer. The diagnosis itself can be traumatizing, and treatment is very hard. It seems there is a lot of bad before the good, meaning a lot of awful side effects from treatment in hopes of ridding the body of cancer. This reality is, for me, even harder when the patient is a young person. The day I met Angela I knew I was in for some heartache.

Her name fit her so well, for she truly was angelic – kind, gentle, other-centered, wise and full of faith in God. She had been married for seven years and had two children, ages five and three. Her husband was equally as wonderful and a good father who had taken the reins when Angela was diagnosed with stage four cancer the year before. On hearing the diagnosis, Angela simply said, "Nothing has changed. Jesus still rose from the dead!" She had proceeded with courage and the same attention to her family she had always had. By the time she came to my hospital, she was very weak but still determined. She spent early mornings and evenings praying and listening to hear God's voice. She listened for direction, for wisdom in caring for her family, for encouragement.

As the days at the hospital passed, Angela met with every discipline to discuss her care. Her husband went home and returned with the children, which brought such joy to Angela. A care plan was put in place and Angela received her first treatment in the very comfortable chemotherapy suite. The next day they left to go home, hoping to beat the onset of side effects. This schedule continued for several months as the new treatment plan went into effect. Each time the children came along to the hospital, the family staying close by in a hotel. They always came to the chapel to play, calling it "the God Room," and I took the opportunity to play, too!

The older child, a girl, was very aware of her mother's illness and the need for treatment. As she understood it, "Sometimes we get so sick we have to go back to God to get better." More than once a visit, this sweet child brought me to tears with her uncomplicated understanding of God and our lives. Her younger brother was less aware of what was happening – he just wanted to play! The three of us talked about their mom, how she loved God, how she loved their dad, how she loved each of them, how she may have to go back to God before they grew up.

Each visit seemed to add a layer of reality as Angela became weaker. The powerful chemotherapy was killing lots of cancer cells, but it was also wearing her down, causing her to lose weight and strength.

After one particularly difficult round, she was admitted to the inpatient unit for more care and observation. The children became a welcome presence on the inpatient unit and everyone made sure they were looked after and made comfortable. Red Jello became a daily treat! The children often climbed up into the bed with Angela for stories, snuggling or a nap. The three-year-old boy was fascinated by the fact that he could push a button and the bed would move up and down and "fold up." He had everyone laughing! These were precious and heartbreaking scenes. Their dad took many photographs for them to look back on as the years passed.

 The main thing I saw in the children was that they had no fear. When they were uncertain, they looked to their dad who held them and talked quietly with them about what was bothering them. They were never kept away from their mother, but were also given clear explanations about how to interact with her so they did not inadvertently cause pain or discomfort or disturb her sleep. Angela's husband worked on ways for the children to spend time with her without causing her physical stress. One day he arrived with a basket full of manicure supplies. Each child took a hand and did their very best to "make Mommy's fingers beautiful!"

 In the meantime, Angela was gaining strength but only because chemotherapy had stopped. She decided she wanted no further treatment. She felt she was losing time with her family and preferred to go home and make the most of the time they had. It was a sad time for those of us who had come to love this dear young family, but we also understood and could see from a distance that it was the right thing. We took more photographs, packed up treats and things to entertain the children on their long drive home, and all at once they were gone. Angela's husband had promised to keep us informed and we promised to keep them close to our hearts.

That afternoon, I went back to the inpatient unit and called an impromptu staff meeting. No one needed to ask why. We sat together, silent at first, then talking about how this little family had touched us. We had all been impressed with the parenting that allowed such young children to handle such a devastating situation. We talked about their faith that taught them to trust God even when they didn't understand. Or possibly, especially when they didn't understand! We talked about the peace Angela had, even at the thought of leaving her babies behind. It was a great time of sharing our pain, while finding encouragement in each other's experiences with this family. We cried, we hugged, we sniffled, we prayed for courage and hope, then we went back to work. We knew we had each done the very best we could for Angela and her little family and now we would turn our attention to the next family.

Over the next four months or so, we had occasional emails updating us on Angela's condition. Things did not look good, from an earthly perspective. Finally the email came telling us she had died. Although we had realized it was coming, many of us still held out hope that she would survive. The email encouraged us as her husband looked to their faith and told us about their hope of heaven and the joy and freedom in God's presence which he believed Angela was now experiencing. He included a photograph of both children, one on each side of Angela in her bed. Her chin gently rested on her son's head and there was an expression of total peace on her face. She had managed to face cancer with strength, yet with trust in God. She had made decisions about her treatment and care after talking with those closest and most trusted in her life, then she had turned her hands, palms up, and asked God to be close to them and give all of them courage and peace and, ultimately, reinforce their hope of heaven.

I continue to reflect back on Angela and her family when I meet children dealing with cancer. Our natural tendency, I think, is to protect children from harsh realities. While I understand that, I also know dozens of children, including myself, who made up their own stories when not given the true facts. Usually those stories are harmful. While real life can be frightening, when any of us has people around to honestly share the experience, a lot of fear is relieved and time can be much better spent. I had learned so much and felt so much joy with this family. I would miss them showing up in "the God Room!"

13

HARD THINGS

ONE DAY A SWEET WOMAN, Sharon, the wife of a patient, came to my office just off the chapel to talk about "hard things that require hard words." She and her husband, Jeff, were fairly new to the hospital, but I had fallen in love with them. Such gentle spirits, so kind and loving — towards each other and everyone around them! They had been married for more than 20 years, after meeting in college. They did not have children based on personal convictions. It was obvious from my first meeting with them that they had deep respect and affection for each other. The diagnosis of cancer was a shock that reverberated throughout the life they had built together. We had several conversations about faith, God's care and several of the "why's" of their situation. They were tiptoeing around the faith issue, but this day Sharon had other questions on her mind.

It turned out that this precious woman wanted to talk about what should happen if her husband died there at our hospital, instead of at their home in Houston. She asked hard questions: How long before they take his body from me? Where will they keep him? How do I decide when to discontinue life support if it comes to that? And probably my favorite, is a person actually gone when they go on life support or when it's removed?

Sharon was very brave. As we talked, I commented on her bravery and she told me, "I just love him so much that, if the time comes and he's going to die, I want to be able to completely focus on him and nothing else." Oh, my heart. This is love — putting the well-being of another before our own, even when it hurts.

We talked for about 90 minutes and Sharon was brave and strong until her last question, which was, "Will he go home with me or will I have to leave him here and have him flown home by himself?" She started to crack, tried to calm herself, but just burst out with tears and deep sobs. I held her tightly as her tears dripped down my neck. I wanted to scream. I hated cancer more and more.

I loved these two people! We spent hours together just getting to know each other, but also talking about the deeper things of life. I admired their perspectives, as individuals and as a couple, and learned a lot from our times together. We talked about death and the future if Jeff died, or if he lived. They were very transparent with their thoughts, both with each other and with me. They had decided to trust me with their fears, apprehensions, and joys they imagined in their future. They had asked me to stay near if things got bad, so I could be with them if and when he died. They said they would need me. I thought they would be fine. My deep, deep desire was that this dear man would live a long time so they would have more time to love each other and show the rest of us how it's done.

I was blessed to have known this couple, to be a part of their life at a time when they were so vulnerable. As much as I hate cancer, it had brought me yet another picture of love and I will always be thankful for that!

14

SWEET ANNA

WHAT A BEAUTIFUL TIME I had with Anna one spring afternoon in the inpatient unit of the hospital. I had the luxury of an open-ended visit, so I could just sit with her and let the time flow.

Anna and her husband had left their home in Ethiopia fifteen years earlier to live in the US. Everything was good for them. They enjoyed their new life, enjoyed the work they did, and rejoiced when their baby girl arrived. Anna began having strange aches and pains and was eventually diagnosed with cancer. She had been in treatment for a couple of years without much progress. They decided to transfer to a different hospital in hopes of better results.

One of the first things Anna told me was that she didn't question her suffering. She believed God is good and knows what is happening. She thanked God at the most interesting moments – moments when I would be less than thankful. She understood and believed in God's goodness – even when it came to the fact that she was 46 with a young daughter and had a vicious cancer. She and her husband were at the hospital for her treatment when her health took a bad turn and she needed to be admitted for around-the-clock care. Their daughter was staying with relatives, where she was blissfully unaware of the pain her mother was suffering.

That first day of inpatient status, I stopped in to see how Anna was doing. She was having excruciating pain in her leg that no medication could seem to relieve. As we sat together, she played worship songs for me – songs in her native language of Amharic. Of course, I couldn't understand the lyrics, but the music was enchanting. Then Anna began translating for me. Her translation became her worship, and the tears began to roll down my face. To see her in such pain with her beautiful hands lifted, speaking words of praise and thanks to God, was almost more than my heart could take in. She reached over and wiped my tears with her fingers, saying, "He is everything!" Holy ground.

For a long time we sat in silence, just holding hands with our fingers intertwined – brown, white, brown, white, brown, white. What a gift it is to have someone with whom it's comfortable to be silent! As we sat, I had an overwhelming feeling of wanting to change her circumstances. I said, "I wish I could take this from you, even for a few hours!" Anna's response was stunning. She said, "Oh no, dear! I understand your kindness, but this is for me alone. God has much to teach me through my suffering, and I don't want to miss any of it!" My tears started again! Such faith, such trust in her God! Holy ground.

A bit later Anna asked me to rub her leg "ever so lightly" in hopes that somehow the pain would ease. AH HA, I thought, finally something I can DO for her! As I sat next to her bed and rubbed her leg, my sweet friend began to thank God for my hands that he had made and was now using to ease her pain. She smiled at me and said, "My sister, you have holy hands!" With Anna, nothing was about what is seen – it was always about God and his movement in her life. She believed that everything starts in the heart of God.

Oh, how I loved this woman! She taught me every day to trust God, to give God free reign in my life and to be thankful for whatever he brings, because it is HE who brings it. God is alive and loving and eager for me to know him – especially in the depths of suffering. Certainly, God had brought her to me, and I treasure every day I had with her. I hoped for many more days ahead, but also understood that Anna was teaching me at every encounter I had with her to look for God's hand, to pray and to trust God a little bit more each day. She was such a gift. I wish everyone could know her. Hearts would be changed, as mine has!

About nine months after that afternoon visit, we received word from her husband that Anna had died. While I instantly felt sadness and deep loss, I also knew that, according to her faith, she was with God and now pain-free. I could not deny her that relief, that joy; I was just sad that she had to go so soon. Another staff member who had grown close to Anna came to my office for a cry. As we sniffled, we talked about how to celebrate Anna, since we obviously could not attend her funeral. We decided to find an Ethiopian restaurant and go for a meal.

That day was bright and sunny. Both of us commented on the joy we felt knowing we were celebrating such a precious soul. We enjoyed our meal, which was very different from American food, and we talked about how Anna would laugh at these two American women eating with our fingers! As it came time to part ways, we took a few minutes to pray and thank God for this woman we had loved and learned so much from. We asked a blessing on Anna's husband and little girl, who would surely be challenged as they adjusted to a life without her. As my colleague ended our prayer with, "Amen," I remembered that the word "amen" means "truth" in Hebrew, the original language of the Old Testament. In that moment I had a very real sense of comfort and well-being. Anna had lived her truth and had died in her truth. She wholly believed God held her life, and that belief gave her great peace to the end. I will always remember that. I will always remember Anna.

15

DEATH AND SUPER GLUE

AS A HOSPICE CHAPLAIN, I go to a LOT of funerals. I always enjoy the various ways families personalize this ritual, this final goodbye to their loved one. There is one funeral, however, that will probably stay with me forever. This funeral was that of a sweet little eight-year-old who died of leukemia. The line outside the funeral home was very long, even though I arrived about 40 minutes early. As I waited, people greeted each other, shook their heads, and cried in each other's arms. Most seemed to have known little Rachel her entire life. I was touched by the love and encouragement I saw. Several people greeted me, saying I didn't look familiar. When I explained that I worked with Rachel's father, it was as if I became part of the family. I listened to their stories about this little girl they loved and came to a deeper understanding of their sadness.

Rachel had been a particularly bright and bubbly child. She was the fourth of her parent's five children and their only girl. She was a very "girly" girl – loved pink and purple, sequins and sparkles, ponies, baby dolls, and baking with her mother. When she was school-aged, she took to her new surroundings without hesitation. She helped the teacher whenever a volunteer was needed, excelled at math, and seemed to be every student's best friend. Rachel thought she wanted to be a teacher one day.

Midway through her second-grade year, Rachel began not feeling well. It was very unusual for Rachel to miss any activity, so when she told her mother she was too tired to go to school, her mother knew something was wrong. A few weeks later came the diagnosis of leukemia. The disease progressed quickly in spite of treatment and before long, Rachel was at home nearing the end of her life. I had followed her treatment, checking in with her father at work and letting him know I was praying for their family. There was nothing else I could do! Their home was a blur of activity with people bringing meals, others helping other children with homework, others cleaning, others talking with Rachel, others sitting with her mother and praying. Although there were always a lot of people, the atmosphere was peaceful. Her father attributed that to the fact that most were people of faith, so they brought peace and positivity with them.

The last few days of Rachel's life, her father stayed at home. At work, several of us gathered in the chapel to pray for the family. Then the call came telling us Rachel had died. While her father was heartbroken, he clung to his strong Catholic faith and believed Rachel was at peace. He told us it was a relief that his girl no longer had to go through treatments, no longer had side effects, was no longer confined to her bed. He and his family were beginning to make funeral plans and would send us the details.

Everything was pink – the casket, the flowers, her fingernails, her lips, and the little Teddy Bear wedged into her hands. I don't care for viewings, although I know they have a valid purpose. I usually choose to go around the viewing line and greet the family. This funeral felt different, perhaps because this was a young child. I wanted to honor her and her family in every way I could.

So, out of respect to the family and their culture, I stood there beside her as her body lay in the casket. Her pink dress was obviously new, with lots of ruffles and sequins. Her beautiful long hair was perfectly in place and she honestly looked very serene. As I stood next to her, wrestling with sadness and questions, I asked God to bring comfort to her parents, to her siblings and community.

Then I spotted the Super Glue that held her eyelids closed. It was almost more than I could take. It was surreal – there are SO many things wrong with an eight-year-old having her eyelids closed with Super Glue; SO many things wrong with her death. My heart ached. When I think of that scene even today, my heart aches. As I walked over to greet her parents, I hoped they hadn't seen the Super Glue. After all, if it had been that painful for me, I couldn't imagine how they would feel.

They greeted me with a warm hug and thanked me for being there. They talked about their trust in a kind and loving God who had decided to allow their daughter early entrance into heaven. Although they already missed her desperately, they were thankful she was safe, peaceful, and forever with her God. Their faith moved me and gave me a lot to consider about my own faith. I wondered if this was a response born out of shock and deep grief, but they remained steadfast in their faith through the next several years.

I came to believe their steadfastness in faith was built on the shoulders of their community. They had loving friends who walked with them week after week after week as the family first dealt with Rachel's diagnosis and treatment, and then her death. The parish community encouraged them in faith, and in the rest of life as well. When one of the "firsts" without Rachel would approach, there was always someone around to talk, pray, hug, or do whatever they needed to encourage them. As I observed from afar, I took mental notes to remind myself of how to love a grieving family. I'm convinced to this day that Rachel's family would have faced a much harder battle without the care of their community. It was a beautiful thing to see!

16

A SAD DAY FOR A GRAVESIDE SERVICE

ANOTHER MEMORIAL SERVICE I OFFICIATED was very different than Rachel's. This was a woman of 86 years who had lived a wonderful life full of travel, adventurous experiences, and a strong family. She had married young (21) against the advice of her parents. They warned her about the possibilities of marrying an older man (30), but there was no stopping her. Her husband was already established in his career, so Ann was free to explore her interests. She had always wanted children and, eventually, they had a son and then a daughter. As they raised their children, Ann and her husband continued to travel on their own, vacation as a family, attend church now and then, play at their monthly "Bridge" group, and generally enjoy life. As the children grew and then went off to college, the pace slowed and Ann's husband retired.

Then, very suddenly, one day he was gone. He had been in the yard "puttering" and suffered a massive stroke. The family was stunned. They did their best to hold together through the funeral week, but things began to falter as Ann made decisions about the house and their decades of possessions. The tension became so severe that Ann's children would no longer be in the same place together nor even speak to each other. This was heartbreaking for Ann, but she was not able to help them find their way back together.

Several years passed and Ann moved into her son and daughter-in-law's home. The in-law suite at their house was perfect for her to remain independent as long as she could and, when the time came that she needed help and care, she could remain at home. She secretly hoped her daughter would visit and make amends with her son, but it didn't happen. Ann died without seeing her daughter again.

I was more than a bit apprehensive at the thought of officiating this memorial service with a feuding family. I had all sorts of pictures in my head of what could go wrong. I spoke with Ann's son and his wife and we planned a graveside service, "lasting no more than 10 minutes!" We had no idea who would attend the service, but I planned to proceed as if nothing was amiss.

As it turned out, it was a sad day for a graveside service. It was cold and gray with wet snow falling. It might have been pretty if we'd been inside by a fireplace, but here by a deep, dark grave it was just awful. I waited in my car until the funeral director waved me toward the forest green tent they had set up with several folding chairs for guests to use. I stood behind the podium, the heels of my shoes sinking into the wet ground, and began to get my notes organized.

Out of the corner of my eye, I saw activity and turned to see what was happening. As I looked around, I realized Ann's daughter and her family must have arrived. Because I had never met them, I wanted to introduce myself. As I did so, I could see tears in her eyes and I hoped she might reach out to her brother in reconciliation. She did not. Her children and her brother's children snuck glances at each other and I could only imagine what these cousins had been told about the other family members. She and her family took their seats and looked straight ahead, looking at me once or twice. The service was very short, as requested, and after I closed with a prayer, they stood up, walked to their van, got in and drove away.

It took me a few days to recover from the experience of this service. There were many layers to it for me and each one was full of emotion. First, children were saying a final goodbye to their mother, the one person who knew them before anyone else. Second, grandchildren were saying goodbye to the grandmother who had delighted in spoiling them so well. Then there was the divide between these two people who had spent their entire lives together. No one else knew the family history or childhood adventures the way they did, yet they were willing to let it all go. Ann's possessions would be divided according to her will, and the family attorney would handle all other details. As far as I know, the divide was never mended. The loss for this family went beyond their mother's death, in my opinion.

17

THE LONGEST FUNERAL

I HAVE LEARNED OVER THE YEARS THAT, if I want to attend someone's funeral to be supportive of their family, it is best to attend what is called "the viewing" or "calling hours" or "family night." All these titles mean the same thing. It is a span of time two to three hours in length when family, friends, neighbors, or anyone else may greet the family and spend time with the other guests. Most often this means the prepared body will be present with the casket open so guests are able to see the person. Many people need this time to help them accept the death, to truly believe the person is dead.

As such, it can be an emotionally volatile time. I have seen women faint, children scream and run away, and one woman nearly tipped over the entire casket as she attempted to reach into the casket and hug the deceased! Even so, it is usually fairly easy to know what is in store for the event and, if things get uncomfortable, it is easy to leave.

Funerals in a church building are not that simple. Most often the guests are seated when the family walks to the front of the sanctuary to be seated. It is usually quiet and orderly with solemn rituals including singing, prayer, a eulogy, and a sermon of some sort. Most services are kept to 30 minutes or less. Most.

I found myself driving to the funeral of a dearly loved patient whose small family had become special to our entire staff. One other hospice staff person was also attending and we planned to sit together. I arrived at the quaint country church and made my way about halfway toward the front of the sanctuary where I took a seat on the cushioned pew. Several people greeted me and welcomed me and the funeral director waved hello (it's probably not good that the funeral directors know me so well!) as I made my way. My colleague soon joined me and the church began to fill. I already had my afternoon visits planned, so I knew how much time I had for the funeral.

Thinking I had planned well with more than enough time, I settled back to whisper-chat with my colleague. Soon the casket was escorted down the aisle and placed in the front of the sanctuary, while the family followed and was seated in their front pews. Among the family members were several small children who were already fussy, and I wondered how the service would play out. I didn't have to wait long. The pastor's booming voice shouted out, "THIS is the day the Lord has made! Let us reJOICE and be glad!" He then said a prayer asking God for comfort and strength for the family as well as all who loved the deceased.

As we settled back into our seats, the organ began to play and a song leader took her place behind the podium. We sang about six songs of celebration and praise to God, a couple of them repeating the last verses several times. Then a man took the podium to read passages from the Bible chosen by the deceased for this service. He then continued with verses he thought would encourage the hearts of those present.

Somewhere between passages, a child of maybe two years ran from the pew and up the aisle, crying the entire way! I could see, in my imagination, the other little ones congratulating him as he ran, wondering if they might have the courage to do the same! He was soon apprehended, spoken to, and brought back to his seat in the pew. By now a couple of other children had started to cry. which seemed to be the cue to the "sound man" to increase the volume.

As we began singing again, the organ was booming. We sang for what seemed like a very long time, then a family member went to the podium to read the obituary. I enjoy hearing patients' obituaries because I learn things about them I hadn't known previously, and this one was no different. As the reader finished, four people rose from their pews and made their way to the front just to the side of the podium. Each person held an instrument and one seated himself at the piano. The hymn was unfamiliar to me, but it spoke of God's love and care for his children and their hope of heaven. When they began playing "Amazing Grace" two voices, almost simultaneously, cried out loudly and began sobbing.

This was the first time I wondered how long the service might last. I looked at my watch to see it had already been nearly an hour and

I had a feeling we were just warming up. I began to wonder how rude it would be to leave. Another thirty minutes passed. I leaned over to my colleague and, after a few whispers, decided to stay. I knew I had a full afternoon and at least had to call to notify them of my situation. The funeral service went on. In the program, there were more readers, two soloists, a grandchild who had written a poem, and more hymns. At least two babies were growing tired. I didn't want to be rude by leaving, but I also didn't want to be rude by being late to my scheduled visits.

After another whispered conversation with my colleague, it was decided that at the next break in the service, we would leave. It took a good twenty minutes to find that break, but we finally made our exit. The service had lasted (so far) two and a half hours. That day, I learned to only go to the viewing/calling hours/family night!

18

IN THEIR OWN SWEET TIME

FOR ME, one of the most interesting aspects of being with people who are in their last days and hours of life involves the actual moment of death. There are, of course, many physiological changes in the human body as death approaches. Eating and drinking slows, then stops, a state of unresponsiveness sets in, extremities begin to mottle, fingernail beds develop a blue-gray hue, skin becomes dry and cool, breathing slows and becomes apneic, and there is a general sense that the individual is no longer "here" but is somewhere close to the next life.

This can be an unnerving time for loved ones, and yet patients are still able to communicate in the slightest ways. It may be the twitch of an eyebrow, the squeeze of a hand, a slight vocalization or a quick wrinkle of the brow, but it definitely happens in response to questions or comments from loved ones. Along this line is the length of time between a patient becoming unresponsive and the time of death.

Much to the dismay of loved ones and friends, there is no way to predict the actual death, and this time period can be stressful. There is so much we do not know, so much unseen where death is concerned, but those dying have taught me the human spirit somehow interacts with the Giver of Life to determine the moment of death. The human spirit is strong and influential as life ends. This can be both comforting and unnerving to those keeping vigil.

Katherine was a young, accomplished businesswoman who had lived her entire adult life in New York while traveling the world and earning an enormous salary. She came to us very weak, but very much in control of her situation. Everything was in place, everything had been planned and paid for. She had spoken with nearly all the people to whom she wanted to say her goodbyes, and she told us her heart was peaceful.

As her health declined, Katherine began to talk about one friend, Alice, that she had not been able to contact. It became increasingly obvious that Alice was important to her and she was frustrated at not being able to locate her. Seeing Katherine's distress, one of the social workers took the most recent contact information on Alice and went to work. Over the next couple of days, Katherine became weaker, declined meals, and was taking only water. We feared Alice wouldn't be found in time.

But then the social worker was given the correct phone number and made contact with her! She told the social worker she would come to see Katherine, leaving the next day to fly across the country. Katherine was unresponsive by this time, and we were not at all sure Alice would arrive before she died. We told Katherine that Alice was on her way and would see her soon.

The next day, with her friend's flight arriving in the afternoon, Katherine was less present than ever. We kept her informed of Alice's progress with reports of, "The flight leaves in an hour," and "The flight is in the air," to "Alice has landed and is in the car coming this way," to finally, "She's here!" It was a joyous reunion as Alice held Katherine's hand, then snuggled next to her in the bed. We all left the room to allow them time alone.

The amazing thing is that within 30 minutes, Katherine died. It appeared she had waited for Alice's arrival to allow herself to relax and die, leaving this world behind. We all stood together in silence, in awe of the strength of the human spirit within Katherine that allowed her to hold on long enough to say goodbye to her friend in person.

This same scenario is one I've witnessed over and over as people die, but sometimes in the reverse. Families often refuse to leave the bedside of their loved one until they absolutely have to, whether it's for a meal, for childcare, a shower, or out of pure exhaustion. So often it is during that time a patient, particularly a parent, will die. The human spirit in that patient will continue to "protect" their child from the pain of that actual moment of death.

I began visiting with a dear woman, 84 years of age, who had moved into her daughter and son-in-law's home as her health declined. Mary was a woman of strong faith and was ready to be with God after "too long" wrestling with declining health. Her daughter Patty, however, was not ready to say goodbye. For several weeks I visited and talked with

Mary who, as is often the case, strengthened my faith! She then asked me to focus on her daughter. Mary feared her daughter was fragile and may return to the alcoholism that plagued her for so long.

Another several weeks were spent talking with Patty. We talked, we prayed, we laughed, we cried, all as Mary declined and then became unresponsive. We would sit with Mary, telling her about our conversations, Patty reassuring her mother she'd be fine, and praying for peace. Mary had been without food or liquids for several days. The hospice staff assured Patty her mother was comfortable, since the body doesn't require fuel as it shuts down. We waited, nurses visiting the home each day to assess Mary's progress toward death.

I visited once or twice a week and spoke to Patty on the phone to provide reassurance that she was doing all she could for her mother. By day ten we were all amazed that Mary was still alive! Her nurse continued to visit, as did I, and we marveled at Mary's spirit even as we searched for anything she may be waiting for before she died. She had had many visitors while she was cognizant, she and Patty had deep conversations about important things, and her son-in-law assured her all her finances were in order. We could not find anything that may be holding her back, so we waited and kept her company.

One morning, day 16 without food or liquids, I called to let Patty know I was coming to visit but there was no answer. This was fairly common, so I went ahead with my schedule. When I arrived at Patty's house and rang the doorbell, there was an unusually long wait. Finally the door opened and there stood a very sleepy Patty with bed-head, droopy eyes, rumpled pajama pants, and a t-shirt. She had had a busy night and had gone back to bed just before the sun rose. We chatted for a few minutes as she told me about the previous night and then she said, "Well, let's go check on Mama!"

As we entered the room, I could see Mary was gone. Patty was arranging the sheets when she suddenly said, "I don't think she's breathing!" I said, "She's not. She's gone." Experience has taught me those first moments are unpredictable, so I waited for Patty to respond. She watched a few more seconds to be sure her mother wasn't breathing and then said, "Well FINALLY, Mama! Hallelujah!" We laughed, then cried, then sat with Mary for a time. We talked about why she had waited so long to go, but came to the conclusion we would never know. It seems there is a fine line between the timing of the Creator and the human spirit – a line we, as humans, cannot anticipate no matter how we try!

Often patients will work hard to get their lives organized and get various things in place before they relax and lean into heaven. I have seen this happen hundreds of times! One such patient became very special to me and continues to this day, although she died several years ago. Upon admission, Linda declined chaplaincy services, saying she was "not religious." This is, of course, everyone's right – chaplaincy is a supportive service. Week after week in our staff meeting, we would receive updates on Linda's physical condition, emotional status, and decline.

One week her nurse mentioned that Linda had been very emotional and stressed over the future of her little dog, who was an ever-present companion. Her adult children did not want him and she feared the dog would end up at "the pound" to be euthanized. I decided I would like to meet the little dog and possibly adopt him. So, even though I was the chaplain, Linda was eager to meet me and discuss the situation.

When I arrived at the house, I found Linda in her room, the door closed so the dog would not wander off into the rest of the house. The room was fairly small, but there was a large bird cage with a parrot squawking. There was clothing all over the floor and the dark wallpaper made it seem like a sad space. As soon as I entered the room the little dog, Toby, began to bark and did not stop throughout the entire visit. Linda was full of questions: had I owned a dog before? Where did I live? Was there a yard? Was it fenced? What was my other dog like? Was he aggressive? Had I ever rolled up a magazine and swatted a dog for discipline (?!)? Would he be home alone? Could I afford a groomer? It went on and on.

Over the course of the next four visits, Linda grilled me, asked for photos of my yard (fence included!), and family. As she grew weaker, the questions became fewer, but they were mostly about me and what sort of dog owner I would be. Linda canceled two visits because she was declining, but then came an urgent call to come see her.

On a Thursday morning, I made Linda my first visit. She was markedly weaker, no longer eating, and sleeping most of the day. When I walked in, she gave me a tired smile and as I held her hand said, "I've decided you can have Toby. Just promise me you won't send him to the pound." We both started to cry and I assured Linda I would care for him until his end. She thanked me and squeezed my hand. I sat with her a while, snuggled Toby, prayed for peace for her and her family, and quietly left the room.

Downstairs, on my way out the door, Linda's daughter thanked me for providing this final bit of peace for her mother. I told her I would be back the following week to check in on all of them and went on my way. Sunday evening, as is my habit, I checked my work email and schedule for the upcoming week. There it was. Linda had died that afternoon. It seemed she needed to have a good home for Toby before she could let her spirit settle and lean into heaven. On Monday morning I went to pick up Toby, and he is still with me today.

Some people question their faith as they face death, and question if God is even real. While I never "beat people over the head with a Bible" I do ask a lot of questions and help them find their own answers. They need reassurance, not debate, and are most often able to reassure themselves when they are helped to clear the fog a bit.

One such woman was Carol, a 67-year-old with pancreatic cancer. This cancer is known to be lethal and quick, usually because by the time there are symptoms the cancer has spread. A colleague called me one day and asked me to visit with Carol, who was declining quickly and was full of fear. She was reportedly a woman of strong faith in God, but could not "find him" these days. I agreed to see her and went to her room the next day.

Carol appeared alert and pleasant, comfortable in her hospital bed with a pretty pink, white, and green floral comforter on her bed. She was quick to get to the questions at hand – where is God? Does he care? Have I done something to push him away? How can I make this fear go away? My heart ached for Carol! She was in a difficult place and had never felt a distance from God before.

After reading her chart I knew she was declining rapidly and didn't have a lot of time. At the same time, I felt a check in my spirit that reminded me not to rush things, to move ahead in the peace and hope God offers to those who want to find him. We talked at length about

Carol's faith, how she came to believe in God, and situations where God worked in her life. She was animated and thorough in her description of every detail of her story.

I could also see her getting tired, so my questions became more pointed: "If God was there for you then, why would he leave you now?" and "What might be distracting you from recognizing God's hand in your current situation?" and what turned out to be the answer to all the questions, "Is there a passage in the Bible that has encouraged you before?" Carol's eyes opened wide and she said, "I've always loved Psalm 23, but I haven't wanted to think about it because I've usually only heard it at funerals!" She smiled at the irony and I asked if we could talk about the Psalm for a minute. Carol agreed.

As I told Carol, I had been required to memorize the Psalm in my third grade Sunday School class. Over the many years since I was in third grade, I had recited it, thought it through and asked questions about it. I asked if I could share some of what I had learned and Carol agreed. The very first verse, "The Lord is my shepherd, I shall not want…" I explained, was all we needed to know to have a peaceful heart if we understood it clearly. When the Psalm was written, the culture of the day was all about herds and crops. Sheep provided a living for the shepherd, but it was his responsibility to care for the herd completely— feed them, water them, shelter them, protect them. So, if God is **our** shepherd, we are safe in all ways!

There was a lovely silence for a bit until Carol said, "That makes sense. I never thought about that!" We continued on talking through the Psalm and Carol seemed to enjoy answering and asking questions. I did, however, feel some apprehension as we approached the "valley of the shadow of death" verse. But there we were: "...even though I walk in the valley of the shadow of death, I will fear no evil."

Carol admitted she had always been confused by this verse, wondering how one could not be afraid of something as vast and unknown as death. Tears fell and fears were faced. Minutes of silence passed. Then I reminded Carol of the rest of the verse: "...because You are with me." The shepherd says he fears no evil because he knows God is with him and, as he said in the first verse, God is his shepherd who cares for him completely!

There was more silence as Carol mulled these thoughts over in her spirit. I could see she was tired, so after a bit more conversation, I prayed for her and prepared to leave. Carol thanked me for coming, for listening to things she'd been afraid to say out loud, for thinking through her favorite Psalm with her, and for praying. I thanked her for her bravery, her honesty, and her willingness to face her fears at such a vulnerable time. It had been a lovely time together and I would be able to see Carol only once more before she died.

As I spoke with her other clinicians, each of them stated a sense of hope and peace in Carol during her last few days. She smiled more readily, squeezed hands as others held on and, before words were too difficult, was more grateful than ever and made sure she told her visitors she appreciated their time. Carol died eight days after our Psalm 23 discussion. Once she had worked through her fears and found hope, she was able to lean into death. I still think about Carol and her Shepherd when I get into difficult situations. We both learned a deeper lesson of faith and hope.

19
I SEE DEAD PEOPLE

THERE ARE SO MANY MYSTERIES when it comes to death. We cannot exactly research what happens after a heart stops and breathing ceases. Of course, there are those who report near-death experiences and, while I find those reports interesting, the person doesn't really have the full experience of death. After all, they return to life! I have long been fascinated by the relationship between the seen and the unseen. I have attended enough deaths that I can identify clues that physical death is near. This can be very comforting to family members who don't understand why their loved one is saying certain things or behaving in certain ways.

Quite often people of faith will talk about "going home." To them, heaven is their home where they will live forever with God and loved ones who have died before them. After months or years of illness, surgeries, treatments, therapies, medications, pain and limitations, heaven is a welcome relief. If a patient is in the hospital or nursing facility, family may be unsettled and upset by their loved one talking about going home. Once it is understood that they are anticipating heaven, others feel relief and can even encourage the patient by reminding them of who might be waiting to greet them as they enter heaven. It can be a time of blessing and even joy as the focus becomes what they believe heaven to be.

Patients often have visions of loved ones who have died in years past. Often it is a parent or spouse. These visions are very comforting and reassuring for the patients as they engage in conversation. I was visiting with a 98-year-old man, Ronald, when he looked past me to an overstuffed, floral chair and broke into a wide grin. I looked around to find no one else in the room, but sat quietly. Ronald continued with a silent smile for several minutes before the mysterious conversation began.

From what I could gather, he was seeing his wife who had died several years before. He told me he had missed her very much! At one point, Ronald looked away from the chair to me and said, "Isn't she beautiful?" I agreed she was beautiful and he turned his attention back to his wife. Ronald had gained such peace, such joy from seeing his wife and talking with her that I could not have interrupted that with my own reality of not seeing or hearing her.

There is so much we do not know about the unseen world, and the bedside of a dying person is, I believe, no place to debate what is real and what is not. These visions may even give us a glimpse of what is ahead for the patient. One woman saw her mother next to her bed and was very comforted. Her mother had been a nurse and always soothed her when she was sick as a child. As she was dying, her mother came to her with sweet, familiar words and gentle strokes on her forehead. The patient's mother told her, "It's time to get on home – everybody's waitin' for ya!" Sure enough, it was less than a week later that the patient died. I had to smile at the thought of her huge family waiting to greet her as she arrived on the other side of this world!

I once met a man who was concerned about the possibility of heaven being boring! He was a man of faith, so he had no doubt that heaven was real and he would arrive there when his death came. He just wasn't sure about how his time would be spent. I visited with him several times, learning about his life, what he enjoyed doing, his career, his family and various hobbies. As it turned out, he was fascinated with plants and flowers and had large, beautiful gardens at the home he shared with his wife and children. He and his wife spent the winter months planning the spring clean-up, what they might plant, what they might change in any of the gardens, whether they should plant more corn in the vegetable garden or not. At the first hint of spring they went to work, side by side, in overalls and gardening gloves, removing dead leaves, branches, trimming edges and preparing the soil for planting. They were meticulous, and the summer would reveal the beauty of all their loving care to the property.

As I visited with the man and as his health declined, he brought up this concern about boredom in heaven. Of course, I could only answer his questions according to his faith which stated he would be busy worshiping God. We talked about what that might be like and he came up with even more questions about the activity. Then one day something amazing happened: his wife came to him in her well-loved denim overalls and pink gardening gloves! He clearly saw her and heard her voice and, although I did not, I could see the joy in his eyes. I sat quietly as the two conversed. The chat lasted several minutes and then she was gone.

The man looked over at me, smiling, and said, "Well, there's my answer!" Of course, I wanted to know every detail and he was eager to share what he had learned from his dear wife. From the one-sided conversation I was able to hear, I knew they were discussing gardening. As it turned out, his wife was also wearing a wide-brimmed straw hat. She told him, "The sun is much brighter and warmer here!" He learned there were endless varieties of plants and flowers, colors his wife had never seen on earth, fruit trees and vegetable plants with perfect produce and no bugs that would harm or kill plants! The man's face brightened and he smiled. He drifted to sleep before we could talk further, but I was eager to hear more.

My next visit found a very different man. He was very weak, but cheerful and full of words, although they came slowly. He was now excited about being in heaven! His wife had assured him he would not be bored, between worshiping his God and gardening with his dearest love, and it made all the difference for him as he faced his remaining days. He had peace.

PART THREE

20

THE HOLLERS

AFTER EIGHT YEARS WORKING in a cancer treatment setting, I felt the tug to return to hospice. I had learned so much from the treatment center and met a lot of wonderful people who went on from treatment to live long, full lives. Some I am still in contact with to this day! But hospice is definitely my first love and I longed to be back in that environment. This meant a move to the south, which was a new adventure for me.

Southern culture is very different from that of the northeast region of the United States and I had some adjusting to do! At first I was annoyed that everyone called me "honey" and "sweetie," even people half my age! I did, however, enjoy the politeness, the kindness and the warmth I experienced when I was out in the community. Often standing in the grocery store checkout line meant a conversation about a product, the weather, the approaching holiday, or many other topics. People seemed genuinely friendly and I began to move past my discomfort to enjoy these new neighbors. As I settled into my role as hospice chaplain, I learned the local roads and "hot spots," and the beauty of the countryside often made me pull over just to take in the view around me.

As I traveled the back roads to see patients and families, I learned about "hollers." A holler is a tiny community set far into the countryside. Folklore would say the term "holler" came from the fact that residents would call out or yell to communicate with the neighbors because they lived so close together. Whatever the history, it was quite an experience to drive into a holler - a bit like stepping back in time.

The homes I visited were in poor condition, some with no running water and only a wood stove for heat. But in spite of the poor conditions, these families were very full of love and kindness and very committed to making sure their loved ones were comfortable and happy. I began to look forward to my holler visits and spending time with these dear people. Their lives were very different from mine, but their spirits were very similar. I was soon called "the lady preacher" or "city girl" depending on who I greeted first. Both were endearing to me!

As we would sit and talk about life, faith, family history, and so many other topics, somehow I always ended up talking about cooking with each of the women. Each woman had her own special way of cooking squirrel, groundhog, rabbit, and possum, along with the more common deer or bear. I was often offered samples to take home for supper, which I understood to be a very generous gift, but I must confess, I couldn't eat it. The sweetness of the gift was dearly appreciated, but I just couldn't do it!

Each family I met seemed to have several pets, both indoor and outdoor pets. Now, I am not a cat person. They're just too independent and aloof for me! But at one home with two indoor cats, one seemed to think I was the best thing ever and would not leave my side from the moment I stepped in the door. The other indoor cat, Button, was the favorite of my patient, the patriarch of the family. She would settle in on the patient's bed and stay all day and all night, only getting up to eat or make a quick trip outside.

As the patient declined over the course of a couple of months, Button changed her behavior. The family reported that she had moved "her spot" from the end of the bed by the patient's feet to further up, by his elbows. Button would often wiggle herself under his arm so his hand was resting on her back. When visitors came, she ran for the bedroom and hid. Once the house was quiet again, she would return to her post with her friend. This pattern went on until the patient died and, after that, Button avoided the space where the patient's bed had been. She would mostly stay under a bed, coming out to eat and run outside. Her friend was gone.

Another holler family had a dog who was very special to them. His name was "Dog." He was medium sized, shed like mad, barked a LOT and licked everyone who came inside. And Dog really loved his Mama! His guard post was at the head of her bed and he rarely left it.

I met the family very close to the end of the patient's life, so I wasn't able to get to know them very well. But as I observed their interactions and the dozens of family photographs, framed and unframed, on the walls, it was obvious there was great love among them. Whenever I was there, visitors streamed through the door of the tiny home. People would move from the living room, where the patient's hospital bed was, to the kitchen area to make room for the next group of visitors. All the while, Dog kept his post. People tried to take him outside or even out of the room, but he would not budge!

One day when I arrived, I noticed Dog was now up on the bed, snuggled in next to his Mama. I was very sure this was an indicator of the patient's status and brought it up in conversation with the rest of the family. I so appreciated their response. They had no doubt that Dog knew what he was doing, that he had such a deep connection with his Mama that he knew her death was very near. The family even made sure his food and water were brought to the bed so he could be with her as much as possible. Dog pressed his body up against his Mama's back and the two stayed together like that until she died a few hours later.

When the funeral home came, Dog stayed on his post and walked out of the house to the hearse and waited as the transporters secured the gurney inside. They each tousled his ears and said goodbye. Dog sat there a bit before wandering off in the trees. He had done a good job of seeing Mama home.

21

DEATH IN THE TRAILER PARK

THERE WERE A FEW SITUATIONS in the holler where I was caught by surprise and found myself in an unpleasant situation. One of our patients was the patriarch of a large family. There were five generations present when I went for my first visit. I was met outside by one daughter and her husband. She was very upset about her father's condition and hoped my prayer time with him would change everything! I promised I would pray with her father, but God would have the final word and he knew best.

As I turned to enter the "double wide" I caught a whiff of marijuana. There were several people on the back deck and a few on the front porch, and as I entered the home I quickly counted eight more.

The man at the entry loudly announced, "Preacher's here, y'all! Preacher's here!" Down the hall a door slammed. Some people went outside. I found my way to the patient at the back of the home. He was an enormous man, lying on his back and struggling for breath in spite of the oxygen being pushed into his lungs.

I introduced myself and he said he wanted to sit up. Another daughter was called to help and after several attempts, he was propped up on pillows and ready to talk. He could only manage a few words before he was completely exhausted. With a few of those words he asked me to pray for his family, for him and that "there won't be no fights!" I began to pray and the patient whisper-prayed along with me, "Please, Lord! Yes, Lord!" I closed the prayer with an "Amen!" and sat with him several more minutes until I was sure he was asleep.

I then loudly made my way to the front of the house to talk with anyone there, if needed. The family was grateful for my time and prayers and said they would be sure to call if they needed another visit. They lived about an hour from my home so, since it was already after 5:00 pm, I secretly hoped I wouldn't be called to come back. Well, I was about one mile from my home when my phone rang. The patient had died and the eldest daughter asked if I would come and be with them. I quickly walked the dog, turned on some lights and headed back to see the family.

When I arrived, I had to park nearly a block away. There were cars on both sides of the street, on lawns, even double parked. I felt a tiny wiggle of uncertainty, but kept walking toward the house. As I walked up the driveway, the eldest son met me and hugged me. He was very intoxicated, but muttered something like, "Thanks for coming." Again, there was the smell of marijuana in the air and people with beer cans outside, inside, everywhere.

As I went into the house, the eldest son said, "Don't let the hole in the wall scare you. He just got really mad and threw the heavy oak kitchen table." I didn't bother asking which "he" threw the table, but I did ask God to protect me! Once in the house, I sat with a few people as they told stories, laughed, and cried. More people arrived, some people left, and eventually the funeral home arrived to remove the body. This took some maneuvering because of the patient's size and the narrow doorways and hallways. I did my best to keep all family members out of the room for as long as possible, and finally the transporters were out of the house.

One of the daughters climbed up on a kitchen chair and yelled, "YO!! We're gonna pray, y'all! Get in here!" then she got down and motioned for me to climb up on the chair so everyone could hear. I had to laugh as I stood on that chair – this was definitely a unique scene. Someone let out a shrill whistle to get people to quiet down and I began thanking God for the patient's life, each person he had touched along the way, the difference he made in so many lives, and the love he had shown his family. All the while there was chatter, hands waving in the air and various voices calling out, "Thank you, Lord!" I finished the prayer with an "Amen" and many voices followed.

As everyone scattered back to where they had been, I headed toward the door then stopped and spoke with the patient's sister to let her know I would be available if she needed support. As I spoke, making solid eye contact, I realized she was in no condition to retain anything I was saying! So, I simply hugged her and walked through the door. As I walked back down the street to my car I thought about how different people and families can be and the fact that there are so many people in the world I would never get to meet if it weren't for my job.

What struck me, along with differences, was how similar people are. I meet people in a very vulnerable situation and they are all different, but the one thing they have in common is love. The sacrifices they make to care for the patient they share with me are unending and amazing, and it's all because of love. I have seen friends and family members put aside deep wounds to take care of someone who is dying. It's a beautiful, profound, and sacred thing. It's one of the many reasons I love what I do!

22

HAROLD

SOME OF THE PEOPLE I MEET are in a very different situation. They have no one to care for them as they decline, and they spend their days alone. One such man was Harold, who lived in a dilapidated trailer in the middle of nowhere.

I met him at the end of summer when everything was vibrant and green. His trailer was set in a clearing surrounded by very tall trees that provided a canopy over his little home. Animals wandered around – squirrels, groundhogs, skunks, deer, and even an occasional bear. Harold loved watching them from his window!

With his health failing rapidly, he was at a loss to know how to get some help. He had a couple of neighbors who would stop in randomly, but his needs became much more extensive than what they were able to provide. One of the neighbors called the Area Agency on Aging and was able to start the process of securing some care for Harold. At first, he objected. He was a very private man who valued his independence and solitude, but he was also aware of his declining health. Hospice was brought in several months later, when it was determined Harold would not survive his current diagnosis.

My first visit was scheduled and I called Harold to check in as to when would be a good day and time to stop in. I had a hard time hearing him because he spoke so softly, but we made the appointment and I was on my way the following day. As I drove deeper and deeper into the countryside, I was struck by the beauty around me, but also the distance from any town or resources. Harold had lived in this area his entire life, so it was all he knew.

Finally, I drove up a driveway to his trailer. I had to take a breath and gather myself together before getting out of my car. Two windows that were visible to me were broken out, with cardboard covering the open space held in place with duct tape. The front steps were decaying and one step had broken through. On the porch was an aluminum turkey roasting pan half filled with pet food. One cat stood having an afternoon snack. At the window on the end of the trailer a small air conditioner hummed, or rather groaned, to provide cool air to what I would learn was Harold's bedroom. The shrubs and trees around the home were very thick, closing in on the trailer and wrapping it closely with branches, vines, and leaves.

I found my way through the growing grass to the front door and knocked. I heard a faint voice say, "Come on in!" I entered the home into a hallway – bedroom and bathroom to my right, kitchen and living room to my left. I called out to Harold again and followed his voice to the kitchen table. There I met the dearest man with the biggest blue eyes I'd ever seen!

Harold was shy, but very polite. He thanked me for coming and offered me coffee. That was the start of a lovely visit which ended with Harold asking me to return for "another chat." Over the next few months, I learned a lot about Harold's life, his family, his days in the Army, his faith, and what he hoped the end of his life would look like.

As autumn ended on the calendar, those of us caring for Harold began to feel a growing concern at the thought of the winter ahead. He had always heated his home with a wood stove, but he was well beyond the ability to even walk outside to bring wood inside. We also had a very real concern about the trailer roof, which was sagging down into the living room and looked as if it would give way at any time. I was chosen to initiate the conversation with Harold about the need to move into a facility where he would be safe and cared for. I didn't look forward to the conversation at all!

The day for "The Conversation" arrived and I prayed, asking God for wisdom and the perfect words. Harold appeared to be in good spirits as he sat at the kitchen table eating his cheese sandwich with a glass of juice. Unfortunately, the roof had sagged even further since my previous visit and I could see the sky where the ceiling should be. Although this was bad, it gave the perfect visual aid for our conversation!

Once the usual small talk was over, I asked Harold what he thought about the ceiling/roof. He gave a weak smile and hung his head. "I know. I know. It's bad. I don't know what to do – this is my home! It's all I know!"

My heart ached as I tried to comfort him, but I also wanted to keep in mind the goal and what was best for him. And so the conversation began. Harold was very brave as he asked all sorts of questions about what it would be like to live somewhere else, what life in a facility is like and how soon he might have to move. I tried to find the balance between not overwhelming him, but still giving him things to think about. I also knew his hospice home health aide would be arriving later in the day and she would continue our conversation.

As we talked, I was aware of the time passing and Harold's strength waning. He was far too polite to ask me to leave, so I finally decided on my own to wrap things up. He thanked me for my time, as he always did, and said he would think about our conversation. I let him know I would return to continue talking next week. As it turned out, Harold decided to move into the facility and the hospice social worker started the process.

When I returned to visit Harold at home, he was just a few days away from his move. He was in surprisingly good spirits as he sat at the kitchen table having the standard lunch of a cheese sandwich and juice. His sister was coming the following day to pack for him and he was in the process of putting aside things to be kept. Everything else would remain in the trailer until "somebody" emptied it.

I asked Harold to show me a few things he wanted to keep. He was excited to share his treasures, but we never got past the first item! He showed me an old newspaper from his tiny southern town, the Memorial Day edition. The old paper fell open to "the right page" which showed an entire gallery of "the local boys" who had served in various branches of the US military. He more specifically pointed out the row that held his picture, along with five other family members. Harold was so proud! He went on to tell me stories of when they returned from their service, and a time or two there were tears in his eyes.

I went to see Harold each day before moving day. He continued to be in good spirits and I promised I would see him the day after his move to be sure he was settling in well. It was a hard day for me. This dear, gentle man was leaving the only home he'd known to live among people he had never met. I comforted myself with the fact that he would be cared for much more effectively than he had been while living at home alone. I looked forward to seeing him at the facility in his new room with all his needs being met.

As I parked my car in the facility parking lot, I took a deep breath and spoke a quick prayer asking God for strength and encouraging words. As I walked down the hall several people greeted me, since I spent a lot of time visiting other patients in that facility. I stopped to ask one nurse how Harold was settling in and she smiled broadly. "He seems really good!" she said. By now he had only been there for 24 hours, but I was happy to hear this report, just the same!

As I rounded the corner and entered his room, there sat Harold in his bed. He had shaved and was wearing soft cotton pajamas on his body and a broad smile on his face! On his over-the-bed table was his lunch tray with… a cheese sandwich!

So far, he was doing well. He told me liked the bed, the people were nice, and he had slept well. We chatted for a time before I knew I had to leave. Hearing this, his chin went down and his breathing quickened. I told him I would be back in a few days. He nodded his lowered head. I asked if he was ok. He murmured and then said more clearly, "Thanks for your help. I always liked your visits back at the house. This isn't home, but it's what I need." I smiled all the way to my car.

23

THE PAPER AIRPLANE COMPETITION

PEOPLE WHO WORK IN HOSPICE are interesting. We are able to face death with confidence as a natural part of life. We have, for the most part, dealt with our own feelings, thoughts, fears, and beliefs about death and are comfortable with people who are working these things out for themselves. Our work can be stressful, but that is mostly because of schedules, paperwork, red tape, etc.

    I worked with a delightful woman, Delores, who seemed to be able to measure the stress level of our staff and then plan an activity to help us release some tension and laugh together. One Wednesday afternoon after our staff meeting, one such activity was scheduled. We looked forward to these times to be together as people, people who didn't have to discuss patient care but just have fun. So there we were, all crowded around the conference table. Delores passed around one sheet of copy paper to each person. We giggled in anticipation! Delores explained, "Today we are having a paper airplane competition! Your task is to build the airplane and when finished we will all go outside to the lawn and fly them. Whoever flies the farthest WINS!"

No one seemed the least bit interested in the reward, if any, for winning! There were several other questions, then the clock started – we had 15 minutes! It was a riotous time in the conference room as people worked and worked, took test flights, then determined they needed to start over. Everyone was very serious about the task at hand, which was humorous in and of itself – highly educated people getting waaaay too intense about a paper airplane! All too soon the timer chimed and we were finished.

Everyone cheered and, again, it struck me how this simple activity had allowed people to relax and be silly for a bit… and we hadn't even gotten to the flying competition yet! We ambled about, making our way outside on that beautiful, sunny day. Delores gave instructions for the lineup and we all did as we were told.

Delores and the hospice director were our judges and they stood what seemed like at least a mile apart from the start line. The first flight was ready to go. Delores yelled across the lawn, "Ready? Set?... GO!!" and we all sent our paper airplanes flying, hoping they would go on and on.

Oh my goodness, the laughter was uproarious! Some airplanes took a nosedive after only seconds. A few more went a bit farther before crashing, and two seemed to fly forever before gently landing in the grass. Someone called out, "Best out of THREE!" We lined up again and flew our planes, then once again!

There were great cheers and congratulations and even a trophy for the winners! We chattered away with the winners asking for their design secrets (as if we would soon be needing paper airplane building skills!) and enjoying the feeling of sore stomachs from laughing. Slowly, things wound down and we returned to the conference room to gather our belongings and get back to work.

The entire "event" had taken less than an hour, but it had done wonders for our team. We laughed together, saw the competitive side of each other, and simply had fun being together. As silly as it seemed at the beginning, it really had been a very productive and healing time for all of us.

24

JAMES

THE FIRST TIME I MET JAMES, I was amazed by his composure in the midst of the intensity of his disease. He was seated in an electric wheelchair and able to move only his arms. On the tray in front of him, he kept a water bottle and his tablet. I soon learned he was an avid reader and always had a list of titles waiting in a queue. James studied to be an engineer after serving the US in the Marine Corps. Needless to say, James liked things in order.

He had been married for decades and had three grown and very accomplished children with several grandchildren coming along. Though not a man of faith, James was interested in my counseling credentials and whether I might be helpful to him and his entire family as they faced his last days. He had no illusions of healing or recovery. He had done what he could early on in terms of treatment, but he had had enough.

These days he was settled into a lovely, newly built house which was designed with his wheelchair in mind. The house had large rooms and wide doorways. Ramps allowed James to go outside to enjoy the woods and gardens surrounding his home. His wife was close by and one daughter had come to stay and help in any way she could.

As it turned out, I had little conversation with James. On my second visit he was arranged in his hospital bed, complete with an overhead bar to help him shift himself. He was soon unable to do even that. The door to his room was to be kept closed and visitors should check in by phone to get his approval for a visit. Even his wife and daughter were required to text before opening the door. As I considered his background, this all made sense. James was used to doing things a certain way and the past several years had eaten away at his ability to do things. He was clinging to the few things he could still control, and his family easily allowed him this.

After my first visit, James had told his wife that he didn't feel the need to have me meet with him. He felt he had all the pieces in order. He had no unanswered questions and felt a certain peace that his struggle with a tired body would soon end. As I talked to his wife, I found out he was right! Down to the last detail, his death was planned. The only item not on paper was the date and time of death! James had arranged for his body to be donated to science so the disease that took his life could be studied. All the details were written out on how to contact the organization and where to send his body after they had studied it. James wanted no funeral, no flowers, no obituary. He saw all of that as "fluff."

On my next visit I spoke mostly with James' wife and daughter. They were a bit frustrated as they thought through James' "final wishes." They wanted a funeral or memorial service where lifelong friends could get together and honor James, but they knew he didn't want it. How might they compromise? I suggested they talk with James and explain their feelings. Funerals and memorial services are not really about the one who has died, because…they're dead!

These gatherings are for those left behind – a chance to share memories, to be with others who loved and respected the one who died, and to mark a sort of turning point from illness to absence. It's the start of a new life. A life without the person who has been central to their lives for so many years. As we talked, James' family was nodding and "hmmm"-ing. There seemed to be new resolve in their minds and they said they would talk with James before my next visit.

Two weeks went by and I went back to visit James and family. He was no longer getting out of bed, he was sleeping most of his days, and was only reading about an hour a day. I always greeted him and asked what he had been thinking about since I last saw him. His answer was always the same, "Not much!"

His wife and daughter had brought up the subject of a funeral with him and they had a lengthy conversation. She advised me not to bring it up with him, so I did not. As we three women talked outside on the deck in the lovely spring sunshine, I encouraged them to take it slowly, talk with each other about what might be a compromise that James found acceptable, and most of all, enjoy every minute they could with James.

As his story ended, James died peacefully in his home with his wife and two of his three children next to him. Everyone felt a sense of relief after the long, difficult time this man had endured. During one of their final conversations about the funeral, James' wife broke down in tears. He became flustered and she apologized quickly. But the display of emotion seemed to strike James in a new way. He pressed his wife for an explanation of her tears. She told him, "It's not about you – you'll be gone! It's about me being with people who knew you, appreciated you, respected you, learned from you, and loved you! I will need them!"

James was, apparently, dumbstruck. He had no idea of his wife's feelings because he never asked her. He simply laid down the "No Funeral Law" because it was what he wanted. He had not considered her perspective, nor that of his children.

About three months after James died, after the researchers had taken from his body what they needed, and after the body was cremated, his family had a "James Party." It was an elegant party, complete with Champagne, hors d'oeuvres, and servers mingling among the guests making sure everyone was comfortable. Everyone was chatting about when they first met James, how he influenced them, and what they had learned from him.

At one point, the best man in their wedding took the floor and gave a bit of a eulogy, then a toast to James. Everyone stayed later than the invitation suggested, but no one wanted to leave. This quiet, intelligent, kind, orderly man had been part of their lives and they all wanted more remembering. Finally people began to leave, and the family hugged each one and thanked them for being with them.

When all the guests were gone, the family sat together in silence. James' wife eventually said, "This was perfect. Your father would approve and I even think he might have enjoyed it!" As they described it all to me a couple of weeks later, I agreed. I thanked them for pressing James and letting him know how they felt. It allowed him to give them one last gift after he died.

25

CHAPLAINCY AND COVID-19

THE FIRST MURMURINGS OF COVID-19 were beginning when I started working with a different hospice. I was in the throes of training, meeting colleagues and finding my way around town while each day the country was getting more information on the virus. Not even three weeks in, my director told me I would have to work from home. I sort of laughed and said, "I'm the chaplain, how do I work from home?" He shrugged his shoulders and said, "I don't really know, but I'm pretty sure you'll figure it out!" That was the start of a very strange two years!

As with the rest of the country, we were figuring out how to see our patients while staying well ourselves and not bringing COVID-19 to our patients. Because a high percentage of our patients lived in facilities, the hospice had to visit according to what each facility allowed. Very few facilities were allowing any visitors and many had patients and residents confined to their rooms, even for meals. For our patients at home, we simply asked what each family preferred and visited accordingly.

Most families didn't want anyone coming into the house unless absolutely necessary, so there I was with 40 hours to fill each week without leaving the house! Our nurses became the source for anything we might want/need to know and each day we had a morning call and an afternoon call to have a review from the nurses. I would take notes on each patient and, after the call, think through each situation and how I might encourage both patient and family. It really was a horrible situation. When I spoke to family members, there were a lot of tears as they talked about not being able to see their loved ones.

Nurses began making appointments with families to have video chats, so everyone could at least see faces. In some cases, this was a gift. In others, such as with dementia patients, it caused too much confusion and distress for the patient to repeat the calls. So families were separated for months and months. As time went by, facilities got creative and began allowing "window visits." Families could come to a ground floor window and staff would bring a resident to see them. The family would call the staff person's cell phone so they could talk and make eye contact at the same time. Of course, this was a complicated, detailed effort and as staff dwindled, it could not continue.

My heart ached for both residents and family members. It was an unbelievable situation. Patients were not eating as well, were growing weaker because they weren't allowed to walk around their floor, and worst of all they were depressed. I spoke to one dear woman on the phone, as it became my only way of communicating with our patients, thanked her for her time and said I would talk to her the following week. She said, "Well, I'm not so sure I'll be here." I asked what she meant and I heard the tiniest sniffle before she said, "I don't want to live like this anymore and it doesn't seem things will change!" I was stunned.

I did my best to encourage her, but I knew she was right – there was no end in sight to the quarantines. I prayed with her over the phone and said goodbye. I'd like to say she turned a corner and did well, but she did not. It was not within the next week, but she died within the month which was much sooner than she might have. I cried with her children on the phone as they thanked me for providing a bit of companionship during that terrible time.

One facility was allowing chaplains to visit, but only in the COVID-19 unit. I wasn't sure how I felt about that but decided I could not stay away. I was given instruction on how to don and doff all the personal protective equipment (PPE), where to dispose of it, where to sit, how to be heard, how long to stay – it was intense. But off I went, covered head to toe with two layers of whatever would keep that virus away! The residents were very happy to see me and thanked me over and over. I prayed with each one and agonized over not being able to hug them close.

Of course I was thankful for the PPE, but it was very warm underneath those layers and I was sweating. I was starting to get cranky when the thought hit me – the staff! They were working at least eight-hour shifts, many were working twelve-hour shifts, in all that PPE. From what I could see, though, no one was cranky; rather, they were cheerful and encouraging to their patients. It was a beautiful thing to be in the midst of.

As I finished with my last patient (and a couple not on our service!)

I made my way to the draped and sealed opening where I would doff my PPE, dispose of it and climb through the barrier to leave. I could hardly wait for a deep breath of cool March air.

Just then I heard a voice calling, "Chaplain! Wait, come back!" I turned to see the staff gathered at the nurse's station in a circle holding hands. It was a precious sight. These dear people were risking their own health to make sure the patients here were cared for and wanted me to join the circle and pray for them. I practically skipped back down the hall to pray! That day has had a lasting impact on my heart.

As I contacted families to inform them of my visit, which I always do, there was deep gratitude and relief knowing their loved ones had been able to talk with and pray with someone new. I was able to go back many more times, and sometimes one of my friends would be gone. As I visited with the others, we would remember that friend in a sort of (very) informal memorial service. Sadly, there would be many more of those, but we did the best we could to grieve joyfully.

Slowly, healthcare workers were vaccinated, then facility residents, and things began to open up a bit. For me it was like walking into a new world. Two years had passed and so many residents I knew from visiting others were gone. New faces took their place and it was like starting over again. Each facility seemed to have a different screening protocol and sometimes it felt like it took longer to gain entrance than to visit a patient! But these protocols seemed to be working and that was the most important thing. It felt like things were beginning to return to "normal."

26

GRETCHEN THE PLANNER

AS FAMILIES BEGAN WELCOMING ME BACK into their homes, I met a lovely woman called Gretchen. She was 66 years old with unmarried twin sons. Her husband had died five years earlier after 35 years of marriage. Her sons had left their jobs to move in and care for their mother as her health declined. They lived in a large, colonial style house with lots of space outside.

At the time, the house was decorated for fall and Halloween. It was obvious someone had put a lot of effort into the spider webs on the bushes, giant spiders on the front porch, carved pumpkins by the door and even a Frankenstein-type figure next to the front door to welcome visitors! As I entered the house, the adventure continued. The dining room had been converted into a craft room with shelves and bins lining the walls and a large table in the center, still stacked with projects. As I took it all in, I was eager to meet this creative woman!

Gretchen's bedroom was pale pink, with lots of lace and ruffles in the curtains and bed linens. Family photos stood on bedside tables and on each dresser. Gretchen sat in a comfortable overstuffed chair, upholstered in pinks, greens, and creams with a touch of lavender here and there. Her bed jacket was also pink and lacy. A soft fleece (pink!) blanket covered her legs. She greeted me with a wide smile and said, "I'm so glad to meet you! Come sit with me!"

During that first visit, Gretchen shared her life with me – a life, she said, that began when she met her husband, Jeff. They had married young and worked hard to be able to purchase the home we were in at the moment. After making the house their own with new paint, carpeting, some new furniture and beautifully manicured gardens, they were ready to expand their family from two to three. Except, three was actually four! The young couple was thrilled to learn they were having twins and the months couldn't pass fast enough for them. Their sons were the joy of their lives and both parents were very involved in every aspect of their lives.

The years raced by and the boys became men, going off to college. Not long after they graduated, Jeff had a serious heart attack and died a few days later. As always, Gretchen planned every detail of Jeff's funeral, a luncheon afterward and as many other details as she could manage. She found her "power" in making lists, writing out plans then checking things off as they were completed. There was a bit of safety, she said, in seeing in writing all the items that needed attention. Gretchen approached her new life without Jeff as another project, and she actually did well with planning. She had even added a span of time she labeled, "Cry Time." That way, she said, she could still check something and not neglect other things by taking time to cry!

About three years after Jeff died, Gretchen was diagnosed with cancer. She described that time in her life as "so annoying!" because she hadn't planned on cancer treatment consuming her life! By the time I met her she had less than six months to live and she had a brand-new list. It consisted of the many things she wanted to do outside the house, along with a list of things she wanted to accomplish inside the house.

Always the mom, she did not want to burden her sons with having to deal with possessions. She had worked through most of the things on her lists and then created a list for her funeral and other details related to her death. One day the older-by-seven-minutes son called and said Gretchen would like to talk to me "soon." Although I wasn't scheduled to see her until the next week, I went to see Gretchen the next day. By then we had become quite fond of each other, hugging on arrival and before leaving, but the house had a bit of a somber, formal feel to it that day.

The four of us sat in Gretchen's room until she said, "Ok boys, I need to talk to Suzanne alone now." As she settled back on her pillows, she closed her eyes and sighed. We sat in silence for a couple of minutes, then she opened her eyes, arranged her blanket, and smiled at me. As it turned out, Gretchen wanted to discuss the details of her funeral service and she wanted me to officiate. I was taken by surprise and became teary-eyed, but Gretchen pulled me back to the task at hand.

By now she was very weak and easily tired, so I knew we had to make the most of our time. It turned out to be fairly easy since Gretchen had already chosen music, readings, ideas for photo displays, refreshments, and details of cremation and how her cremains would be handled. Since they had not had a service when Jeff died, she wanted their cremains combined and placed in the bottom of a hole where a young tree would be planted.

We met once more to go over everything, although she had created a perfect plan. She seemed comforted to go over things again, and I was happy to spend the time with her. She became unresponsive about a week later. I visited several more times, making sure her sons were doing ok and just sitting with Gretchen and sharing a few words when they came to me. I thanked her for allowing me into her life and home, for showing me courage in motion, for caring for her sons as best she could. I held her hand and cried at the thought of all she had been through, then the reality that soon, according to her faith, she would see Jeff again.

One morning the phone rang too early for anything but bad news. It was Gretchen's younger-by-seven-minutes son telling me she had died. He asked me to come before the funeral home removed her body, so I quickly got ready and left home. Both of Gretchen's son's had puffy eyes and tear-stained cheeks and the sight of them brought me to tears, too. We had a group hug and then went upstairs to sit with Gretchen.

She was wearing her typical pink-with-frills fleece nightgown and as we three sat there, it became very evident that she was just not there anymore! It was as if God had said, "Come on home, Gretchen, and leave that tired and sick body behind. Wait till you see what I have for you here!" At a certain point, one of the sons asked if we were ready to call the funeral home transport team and it was decided it was time.

I always suggest family members step into another room while the transport team does their job, because it can be very emotional to see a loved one being wrapped and taken away. Gretchen's sons agreed and stayed downstairs until the body was secured in the funeral home van. They went out one last time, just to be sure…of what, they didn't know, but just to be sure! And then she was gone.

We three went back into the house and flopped onto the very comfortable sofa, me in the middle with a twin on each side, and just sat together. After a time, I needed to leave so we took time to pray, think about what needed to be done that day and say goodbye. I would call the next day to check in.

The next day we talked at length about the service details. Gretchen's sons had never planned a funeral before but they knew what they did NOT want it to be. We had to consider COVID restrictions and preparations, and the funeral home had instructions as well. It was important to let guests know what was expected so they were allowed to attend. It was eventually decided I would facilitate and lead the guests in a time of memories and reflection. Guests would have the opportunity to share thoughts and we would listen to Gretchen's three favorite songs with a slide show. The room would have tables holding photos, artwork, needlework pieces, poetry Gretchen had written, flowers, and tiny memory cards to take home. We laughed and commented that Gretchen would be proud of our detailed planning!

The obituary was published in the local newspaper and people living at a distance were emailed. The food, beverages, cups, plates and napkins were ordered. I worked on the eulogy and the day was fast approaching. I talked with the sons to see how they were doing. One son was in good spirits, while the other was dreading the funeral and, as he called it, "the final goodbye." We talked for quite a while, and he realized it would be a difficult day but he could keep moving forward.

Finally the weekend of the service was upon us, along with a major snowstorm! We had faced the week with one eye on the weekend weather and, when I talked to the older son, we laughed that we hadn't planned for bad weather! The funeral home notified as many people as possible and family members gathered to make calls to let people know the service was canceled.

The funeral was rescheduled for two weeks ahead. We went through the details again, checked catering orders and anticipated the emotions of the day. Then, mid-week, one son began feeling poorly. He kept it to himself until he couldn't any longer. COVID.

Unbelievable. We canceled again! This was like a bad dream, but we kept moving forward and the next date came along just fine. No weather emergencies, no illnesses, nothing but a clear path. A nice stack of masks for those who may have forgotten to bring one. The sun even shone!!

As everyone gathered, there was a common theme that became obvious. The people who knew Gretchen best commented on the scheduling issues and how she would laugh at her sons' efforts! In fact, Gretchen's attention to detail was a consistent comment that was brought up as friends and family shared their memories of this dear woman. There were a lot of tears and a lot of laughing, and most certainly respect, love and appreciation for the woman we were honoring that day.

In fact, the guests went on talking for so long that the funeral director stepped into the room to signal that we needed to finish! We had a moment of prayer and thanked God for the gift of this amazing woman, then people began to leave. It had been a very good time, with all the details covered. Gretchen would be proud!

CONCLUSION

I HAVE COME SO FAR and learned so much since I was 18 and desperate for a kinder model of caring for the dying than was in place at the time. I have read a crazy number of books on anything related to dying, death, and the death industry. I have read about the theology of death, the care of the dead, support of the bereaved, new and "better" ways of handling remains, and seemingly every other angle on death. I have gone to conferences, webinars, support groups, and one-on-one meetings to learn from people I respected. But the most important thing I have done is to go to work!

My patients, along with their caregivers and families, have taught me the most important lessons when it comes to dying. They have had enormous credibility because they were experiencing the process firsthand. They chose to allow me into their process and I have been profoundly honored by their generosity. It's very much like I have lived in two worlds: one at work with the dying and their families and caregivers, and another world of the living where the days are full of things that will fade away. As I do life in the world of the living, I am often asked how I can do the job I do. My response has been the same for decades: "Dying people are the most fun of anyone!" I usually get a confused look as the subject changes...

I have done a lot of thinking and reflecting on the reality that dying people *are* the most fun! Of course, there are some people who are fearful, anxious, and isolate themselves, but this is not the typical situation. So, why is working with the dying not sad? I think it's a fairly simple reason. Dying people have done the inner work of accepting that they are dying. This seems so basic and uncomplicated, and perhaps that is why it has a profound and freeing effect on people.

As we go through life, we all have the general understanding that people eventually die. We just don't believe death will come to us. Unless someone dies a very sudden death, there is time to tie up loose ends and bid this world goodbye. In my role as chaplain, I have the privilege and joy of supporting people with those loose ends. I get to sit on a hospital bed and ask hard questions, then see a light go on as a patient comes to a conclusion that brings peace and hope.

And this can happen over and over as we work through various aspects of life. Relationships, finances, faith, legacy, possessions, care of the body after death, and so many other things. Each conclusion is like a layer of an onion that is peeled off and thrown away, leaving a lighter onion behind. Finally the layers are dealt with and the dying person can just sit back and relax, enjoying the people around them and whatever level of activity they are able to handle. People of faith are particularly eager for that last day, as they have the hope of heaven in the forefront of their minds. We must not discount the "visits" from long-dead family members which encourage people toward death. These visits are a gift to the dying!

Working with dying people is, I think, the ultimate gift we can give a person. We are facing a part of life most people don't want any part of. In fact, there are many people who will not even visit a dear friend in their last days, nor attend their funeral. Those of us who step close find ourselves blessed and filled with joy, hope, peace, and anticipation as we face death with another. Of course, it can be sad to face the death of someone we love. We will miss them and feel the gap in our lives. But when we are able to give a person the type of death they want, knowing they are dying no matter what, we receive a unique joy.

The reality is, we are all dying. When we are present for one another as our loved ones die, we learn a little bit more about the end of this life and how we want our own end to happen. It is a profound honor to be present when someone dies. For me, it is a stunning moment after which nothing is the same.

When I was a child my dear Aunt Bea, of whom this book is in honor, lived four houses away. She loved me so well and always made me feel like the most important kid in the world. I spent a lot of time at her house doing projects, learning to type (long before computers!), and always having fun.

Sometimes I would be involved in something and suddenly notice it was dark outside. Even though we lived in a tiny neighborhood in a tiny, safe town, the darkness held a lot of uncertainty for me, as well as the certainty that a terrible monster would jump out and swallow me whole! But my Auntie Bea knew me and loved me, so she came up with a plan. She would walk me down the sidewalk to the street and as I ran home, she would go inside and stand by the light switch connected to their porch light. When I got inside my house, I would flash our porch light a few times, then she would flash theirs. We were safe at home!

Several years ago, I read a quote on a card sent to me by a family of a patient. Ram Dass, an American spiritual teacher, said, "We're all just walking each other home." All those years ago, Auntie Bea "walked" me home and then I helped walk her home as she died of cancer. I spend these days walking people home and learning from them as I see their faith, their courage, their joy, their hope, and their humor. It is an amazing calling and I wouldn't want to miss any of it.

Made in the USA
Middletown, DE
23 November 2022